Ordinary to Extra-Ordinary

Ordinary to Extra-Ordinary

Achieving Remarkable Career Success
through Passion, Purpose, and Preparation

Pattie Dale Tye

Forbes | Books

Published by Forbes Books, Charleston, South Carolina.
An imprint of Advantage Media Group.

Forbes Books is a registered trademark, and the Forbes Books colophon is a trademark of Forbes Media, LLC.

Printed in the United States of America.

10 9 8 7 6 5 4 3 2 1

ISBN: 979-8-88750-312-7 (Hardcover)
ISBN: 979-8-88750-313-4 (eBook)

Library of Congress Control Number: 2024901140

Cover design by Matthew Morse.
Layout design by Megan Elger.

This custom publication is intended to provide accurate information and the opinions of the author in regard to the subject matter covered. It is sold with the understanding that the publisher, Forbes Books, is not engaged in rendering legal, financial, or professional services of any kind. If legal advice or other expert assistance is required, the reader is advised to seek the services of a competent professional.

Since 1917, Forbes has remained steadfast in its mission to serve as the defining voice of entrepreneurial capitalism. Forbes Books, launched in 2016 through a partnership with Advantage Media, furthers that aim by helping business and thought leaders bring their stories, passion, and knowledge to the forefront in custom books. Opinions expressed by Forbes Books authors are their own. To be considered for publication, please visit **books.Forbes.com**.

This book is dedicated to my parents, Olema and J. Y. Wilson,
who raised me to be confident and caring and
to always remember the needs of others.

This book is also dedicated to my husband, Jim Tye, without whom
there would be no wind beneath my wings. He has been the steady
hand at the small of my back and the smile that made everything turn
out just right. Deepest thanks to you, my forever young Jim Tye.

CONTENTS

When Pattie Dale asked me to write this foreword for her book, I immediately said yes due to the respect I have for her as a colleague, but more importantly, as a person. After realizing what I had agreed to, panic began to set in. I've never written a foreword and didn't want her inspiring book to get off to a poor start. After conferring with Pattie Dale, searching Google, and taking a trip to Barnes and Noble, I took a shot. I hope it works.

I first met Pattie Dale in 2005 in my outer office at Humana. People hated my outer office. A six-foot-long banner with "that which does not kill you makes you stronger" probably didn't help. When I met her, I was Humana's Chief Operating Officer, and Pattie Dale was interviewing for a Commercial Market CEO role in Houston. For those of you who aren't familiar with Humana, it's a health insurance company.

Before the interview, as I read Pattie Dale's resume, I wondered why we thought she'd make a good health insurance market CEO as her prior experience included life insurance sales, time as a manufacturer's rep, and working as an executive at a telephone company. After an hour with her, it was apparent why she was sitting before me. It was clear she had done her homework and already knew a great deal about our business and Humana. She was passionate about how her past experience would make a contribution to the role she was seeking. Finally, and most importantly, her positive and can-do attitude made me want to be around her (and find more people like her). She took the job despite having to stare at that six-foot banner during our time together.

My intuition about Pattie Dale was quickly confirmed. At Humana, we performed quarterly market reviews where market CEOs and their leadership team review their Annual Plan and the progress against that plan. In transparency, these reviews were probably difficult for the presenters with questions coming from all corners. In fact, I've heard these reviews referred to by some as a "skeet shoot."

As she began her review, at some point, I asked if I could ask a question. Her reply set the tone for the whole meeting when she said, "I wish you wouldn't and wait until the end." By the end of the meeting, it was clear that after a few months, Pattie Dale had things under control. The Houston turn-around was under way.

Throughout her Humana career, we turned to Pattie Dale to take on challenging new responsibilities that might otherwise be difficult transitions for many. In each instance, she attacked the challenge. She shifted from a market CEO role to leading our entire commercial line of business. Then we shifted her into a senior Medicare line of business role. You name it, we created the "opportunity."

In one such challenge, Humana's CEO, Bruce Broussard, wanted to better understand the drivers of health in the communities Humana served and how to proactively address those health drivers before they impacted the health of our members. We created the program name "Bold Goal" and chose San Antonio as our pilot market. Over a six-month period, Pattie Dale was tasked with creating a strategy and tactics to stitch together health organizations (public and private) to support members' health outside of the typical "sick care" system.

Before long, she had created an integrated and comprehensive network of organizations that Humana partnered with to serve the needs of the San Antonio community. Her efforts were showcased at a Humana leadership meeting in San Antonio, which was capped off by Henry Cisneros, the Mayor of San Antonio at the time, thanking Pattie Dale for the amazing work she had done. It was time for a "Happy Dance." Humana continues to monitor the positive impact of its Bold Goal efforts in San Antonio and its other markets.

So, why did Pattie Dale ask me to write the foreword to her book? Beats me, as I like to say, "I'm just a boring accountant." I have been fortunate to have an almost fifty-year rewarding career, albeit this means I'm hitting my approach shot to the eighteenth hole. During this journey, I have learned and developed a number of guiding principles, which I thought I'd share because they align so well with those included by Pattie Dale in this book:

- Make sure you and everyone around you are having fun.

- Find and develop "foxhole" buddies throughout the organization (people who have your back and know you have their back).

- Come to work every day trying to make (fill in the blank company) better.

- Things take time. It's a journey, but if you keep at it and don't get discouraged, positive results happen.

- If you add value, your efforts will be rewarded.

- Always have a "glass half full" attitude. If your associates and colleagues see you discouraged, they will become discouraged.

- Be curious. Don't look at the "what." Find the "why."

I guess I shouldn't be surprised by the alignment of my principles with those presented by Pattie Dale as the Humana team (obviously including Pattie Dale) worked together to develop them as a part of our amazing culture.

I thought I'd share one final story which helped shape my professional life. In 1999, Humana was experiencing some very bad times. Our share price of $4-$5 (compared to about $450 as I write today) proves my point. At that time, as CFO, I would share where we stood with David Jones, Humana's founder and chairman. At one such meeting, I shared particularly bad news with David; I'm sure David could see that dealing with these problems was impacting me physically and mentally.

When I was done and expecting to hear David's disappointment, David looked me directly in the eye and said, "Jim, the sun will come up tomorrow."

When David said that to me, I immediately realized that "one thing" (see *City Slickers*) would change the way I approached the day-to-day. David was an unbelievable man and mentor.

One final note on the effect Pattie Dale had at Humana: we were not where we needed to be with women in senior leadership roles. To address this, Bonnie Hathcock (Humana's Chief Human Resources Officer) created the Women in Leadership program. Remarkably, Bonnie asked me to be its Executive Sponsor. I recall being shocked and asking Bonnie if she was sure Genghis Khan should sponsor Women in Leadership. Much to my surprise, serving as the Women in Leadership sponsor is in the top five of my most memorable career experiences.

Pattie Dale and the other ten or so women in the first session volunteered to be the "ambassadors" of the program. With no thanks to me, these ten-twelve ladies created one of the most successful leadership programs at Humana. I recall presenting before five hundred or so Humana leaders publicly thanking these "trail blazers" for their efforts. I'm not certain whether the program has survived through today. I do know that the leadership network created during those ten or so years on the "trail blazer" leadership is alive and well today. Another "Happy Dance."

As I read Pattie Dale's book, it took me back to that one hour in my office and what I saw during that hour: can-do, resilience, positivity, grit, reinvention, trust, balance, and fun. As all of you enjoy the book, I'm sure all of you will see what I saw in my outer office. This book is a useful tool regardless of what stage of your career you find yourself. Following Pattie Dale's playbook will enable the reader to develop the skills necessary to experience career success.

A final note: the book is titled *Ordinary to Extraordinary*; unfortunately for me, I never got to know the "ordinary, 98 percent Pattie Dale."

Jim Murray
Former Centene Chief Transformation and Operating Officer

ACKNOWLEDGMENTS

Becoming

You become. It takes a long time. That's why it doesn't happen often to people who break easily or have sharp edges, or who have to be carefully kept. Generally, by the time you are Real, most of your hair has been loved off and your eyes drop out and you get loose in the joints and very shabby. But these things don't matter at all, because once you are Real, you can't be ugly, except to people who don't understand.
—THE VELVETEEN RABBIT

Courage

Courage doesn't always roar. Sometimes courage is the quiet voice at the end of the day saying, "I will try again tomorrow."
—MARY ANNE RADMACHER

Lessons

Some people come in your life as blessings;
others come in our life as lessons.
—MOTHER TERESA

Goodness

Do all the good you can,
By all the means you can,
In all the ways you can,
In all the places you can,
At all the times you can,
To all the people you can,
As long as ever you can.
—JOHN WESLEY

Thank you to so many very kind and generous people who helped me become Real, who taught me quiet courage, who were my blessings and my lessons, and who taught me to do all the good I can:

Jim Murray • Angie Labove • Damon Casemore •
Mike McCallister • London Roth • Bill Tait • Larry Bell •
Carly Fiorina • Gail McGovern • Tony Chase • Gary Goldstein
• Bruce Broussard • Roy Beveridge • Doug Barr • AJ Singleton
• Doug Ballantine • Deb Clary • Heidi Margulis •
Richard McDugald • Mary Logan • Morgan Smith •
Jack Finlayson • Ellie Francisco • Leigh Ann Barney •
Randy Bufford

INTRODUCTION

Over the years, I've had countless conversations with people who are starting their working professions or reentering the workforce after a defined absence and seasoned professionals who are entering the "third stage" of their careers and have more to give and share.

I can identify, sympathize, and empathize with people at these various stages because I have successfully navigated the first two chapters of my career and am building a successful third stage by helping businesses and individuals grow and thrive. What I've found to be common within these three stages is that there is often a lack of a clear pathway to navigate them successfully. Not knowing what is ahead can be an intimidating, lonely, and even scary proposition. I know this from personal experience, but you don't have to walk this path alone. I'm here for you, which is why I wrote this book! It is an honor and a privilege to share thirty-plus years of career life learnings with you. I have walked the path from individual producer to chief operating officer to board director, with many stops along the way. I'm here to help you—authentically!

Your career, key relationships, and health encompass the three longest "paths" you will take throughout your life, and all three interact and impact each other. For a relationship like marriage, you can turn to a pastor, priest, or counselor for wise advice. For health, you can download an app, join a gym, or hire a health coach. But when it comes to your career—whether starting, reentering, or knowing you have more to give—whom can you turn to? Yes, there are "career advisors," but they haven't necessarily walked in your shoes. I have.

Your career choices, and when you make them, are an amazing part of your life's journey. Having a successful career—and we need to keep in mind that *success* means different things to different people— will enable you to live the life you want to lead and to give back and help others in so many areas of life. In Meg Jay's book *The Defining Decade*, she reminds us that 80 percent of life's most crucial decisions are made before age thirty-five.[1] Career choices are among the most important decisions you will make, as those decisions will impact 100 percent of your life!

Too often, people have a "My job is nine to five" mentality. Or "I can't wait for the end of the week … and to end my thirty-year career so that I can move on with life." But if you have the right perspective, your career—no matter what direction it takes or how many roles and titles it includes—can enable you to have meaning and purpose and to use your gifts and talents in extraordinary ways.

My goal is to help you see the treasure you are holding. If you are at the start of your career, the world is your oyster, as the saying goes. For those reentering the workforce, I want to help you remember and then reimagine your career using the skills and experience that will set you up for success. And for those, like me, who are in the third stage of their careers, the world needs you! It needs your skills, wisdom, and experience.

As you read this book, there is a universal principle that I'd like you to keep in mind: let each of you look not only to your own interests but also to the interests of others.[2] This is the foundation that I want to build from. No matter where you are in your career, if you are always looking to help others achieve their goals, you are giving back, and you will reap the rewards for that generosity during your lifetime.

I cannot stress this enough. From the day you graduate from college through to your third career stage, you will meet hundreds, if not thousands, of people. Cherish them, and maintain contact with as many people as possible. This will build your network, which is one of the most important aspects of your career. Today, this is *so* easy to do! I regret I didn't do this *early* in my career, but I have learned the value of this precious asset, and I can tell you unequivocally that my network relationships are one of the most valuable aspects of every-thing I've done. Your network is the place where you can give and receive—notice the order—which is advice I wish I had been given.

To Those Starting Out

As you begin your career, you may see yourself as I was at the beginning of my career.

I was short-term focused on success. I was looking for the quickest—and most often the easiest—path that would move me up the corporate ladder year to year. But the truth is, I felt like I was in a pinball machine, and I got bounced around by whatever "lever"—job opening, department promotion, etc.—was closest to me. Certainly, I had gifts and talents, was gaining experience, and had the drive to succeed that others were looking for. I was also blessed to have people in my life who saw my potential and kept lifting me up and giving me opportunities. But looking back, if I were to give the younger me any career advice, it would be this: "Relax, enjoy the journey, and don't be in such a rush. Enjoy the fact that you have this field of learning opportunity in front of you, and take it all in."

But here's another important point I would tell the younger me: "Never miss a contact or the opportunity to form a new relationship. From day one, you have the opportunity to build and support others through your network of relationships!"

To Those Reentering the Workforce

If you have taken some time away from your career and are now ready to jump back into your work life, I advise you to take some time and journal in detail where you've been. You have created years on your career path, you've stepped out of it, and now you're stepping back in. But before you do, it's important to reacquaint yourself with all the great things you've accomplished, the new skills you've acquired, and the education you have received from life itself. You need to do this for yourself, because it's way too easy to downplay or minimize your experiences, and the tendency to lose confidence will nip at the corners of your mind.

It isn't the norm to take a career break and follow a temporary divergent path. But you were brave enough to do so, and you are even braver to continue your career journey. It's vitally important that you do so with confidence, with your shoulders held back, with your head held high, and with a readiness to tell anyone and everyone who you are! This will negate the inclination to feel "less than."

Once you restart your career, it is important for you to understand that you might feel a little out of sorts. The workplace and environment have no doubt changed in the time you were away. I advise you to have a first-one-there, last-one-to-leave mentality so that you can build your "work legs" and credibility again. Give yourself ninety days, and you will be amazed at yourself!

To Those Entering the Third Stage of Their Career

At this point in your work life, you have gained a tremendous amount of education and experience. And you may be wondering, *What's next? What do I do with all that I've learned?* You are not ready to retire, and you have the drive and energy to continue to work. Begin to consider the mentoring and/or consulting opportunities before you. Think about how your education and experience can promote you into higher positions that you may have disqualified yourself from earlier. Perhaps you are ready to step out of your current job and into your own business, or help advise others who are starting their business. There are unlimited choices and paths ahead of you, and the great thing is that you get to *choose* where you want to go! If you still have it … use it!

• • • • •

I trust my words have excited you. In fact, I hope I have fired you up! Now, turn the page, and together we'll figure out what you want to do and where you want your career to take you, no matter what stage you are in.

Here's to lighting up your career!
Pattie Dale Tye

CHAPTER 1

Shout-Out to the 98 Percent

And will you succeed? Yes, you will indeed!
(98 and ¾ percent guaranteed.)
—DR. SEUSS, *OH, THE PLACES YOU'LL GO!*

I f you are reading this book, chances are you are just about to embark on this magical journey of your career, or you may be reentering your career journey or even in your third stage. And you're likely wondering how you can navigate this adventure to make it as successful as possible. You might also be just a bit intimidated by all you read on social media about how fabulous everybody else is and may think you are not ever going to be as successful as the rest. But hear this: you are special, you can succeed, and you can have an extraordinary career—even if you feel you are not part of the top 2 percent in your class, your sport, your income, or your SAT and GMAT scores.

This puts you in the 98 percent club—the same club I started in, along with almost everyone else in the working world. And that is why

I want to give you a shout-out! I want you to be recognized for who you are and not what society says you are. You are amazing, and you are enough! You are more than enough to have an extraordinary career.

Having an extraordinary career starts with determining what "lights you up." In other words, what are you most passionate about? What stirs you up every time you think about it? For instance, if protecting the planet lights you up, then you cannot ignore that. If innovation excites you, then you must follow that path. If it's helping others live better lives, improving a current product or service, or traveling to foreign countries to help the less fortunate, then you must follow that "light." Keep in mind that what you're most passionate about isn't determined solely by your aptitude or ability. Most often, passion is about what sets your heart on fire and what drives your imagination to explore the "What if?" and the "Why is that?" and the "Is there a better way?"

A Little about Me

I can unabashedly say that I have, and continue to have, an extraordinary career.

I can also unabashedly say that by the world's terms, I'm nobody extraordinary. I had an incredibly normal childhood and a normal education, and in my view there was nothing really special about me when I began my career. Neither in high school nor in college did I receive awards for being a top student; I only made the dean's list once, and I didn't last in Beta Club as long as my friends did. I wasn't a top athlete and only a marginal pianist and vocalist. In my formative years, I was never in the top 2 percent of anything, so I can fully identify with everyone in the 98 percent club!

The first time I really considered being in the top 2 percent of anything was during a conversation with my then boyfriend, now husband of thirty-three years, Jim Tye. We were having a lovely picnic lunch when he turned to me and asked, "What do you want out of life?" I replied, "Hmm ... I want to be in the top 2 percent." At the time, I was referring to being the best of the best in my career and making the most money I could possibly make.

At that time, I had my sights set on succeeding with AT&T and wherever life would take me. I knew I wouldn't be at the *very* top of the charts, but I also knew I wanted to try to get as close as possible ... 2 percent, here I come!

An interesting side note: just a few years later, I would be admitted to AT&T's Leadership Continuity Program, a development program for the top 2 percent of AT&T's employees destined to make it to corporate officer level.

To reach that 2 percent spot, I knew I would have to *work* very *hard*. Nobody was going to hand me a new opportunity or a promotion simply because I showed up. I bring this up to you because in today's world, viewed through the lens of social media, it looks as if *everyone* else's life is perfect. Everyone else is already in the top 2 percent in looks, relationships, academics, and careers. I assure you they are not, but I also assure you that if you lean into your gifts and talents—if you use them to the best of your ability and continually develop them—*and* you work hard, you can get to the top 2 percent in your career!

• • • • •

One of the early keys to my success was having a very loving and supportive family environment, which felt very normal back then. I now see that our normal family was a precious gift. However, if your life has been anything but "normal," you still have an amazingly bright future ahead of you! And the one thing that will truly lift your future's trajectory is your positive attitude—your attitude toward yourself and others. Stay positive, stay resilient, work to be confident, and try never to see yourself as a victim.

While growing up, I was always encouraged to have an attitude centered around doing my best. Not going to college was *not* an option, and I was certainly encouraged to have some type of career. As I look back over my thirty-plus years, my career path did not follow a defined path. Yet I never shied away from the "not knowing"; I approached it with confidence, as if the unknown future was a gift. This gift was full of possibilities and full of "What ifs?"

I encourage you to see the unknown that you are facing as a gift—no matter where you are in life or what your circumstances may be. Don't let social media, the dictates of culture, news about college entry scandals, or the opinions of others deter you from your goals. Even if you are not in the top 2 percent of your class—intellect, athletics, aptitude, etc.—you can get there; you just have to keep an energetic and positive attitude; be willing to put in the time, effort, and work; and stay resilient.

I'm the youngest in a family of loud and happy people. From a very young age, I filed away life learnings that would later enable me to have great success in my career. For example, during evenings around the family dinner table, I learned the value of listening and absorbing rather than reacting. Being the youngest, there were many times I simply didn't get what my family was chattering on about. But I listened and learned! And my vantage point as a listener allowed me to learn as much about what *not to do*—i.e., operate anything that breaks down frequently, such as boats, tractors, my father's old Jeep—as what *to do*, such as go to church without complaint, and don't quit before you are finished. Eventually, I was able to join the conversation as the "listened to" person. But this didn't happen until I learned how to truly add value to the conversation.

"You don't have to be the smartest or the loudest at the table to have a seat at the table" was one of the valuable lessons I learned from family gatherings. Take the time to listen, learn, and prepare, then speak. Always remember to appreciate the value of initially listening more than speaking, absorbing rather than reacting. Then you can add value to the discussion and become the person who is listened *to*.

As I look back over my life, I see other traits in my DNA that have helped shape my career path. For example, I have always admired risk takers and impact makers, whether they were in business—I think of Steve Jobs, Carly Fiorina, Ariana Huffington (*Huffington Post*), and Sara Blakely (Spanx), to name a few—or historical figures such as Lewis and Clark (American explorers) or Neil Armstrong (the first man on the moon). These people, and countless others like them, were willing to take risks, to see the unknown as a gift, and were driven by the ability to make a lasting impact on society. They had a strong vision of whom they wanted to be and where they wanted to go. And along the way, they embraced the fact that everything they did was for the greater good, not just for personal satisfaction.

I was also a risk taker and was willing to welcome the new, new thing. For me, that new, new thing always revolved around business. I watched my father grow his insurance business and achieve success but never rest on his laurels; he, too, was looking for the new, new thing. I recall sitting in his huge office chair, pretending I was the one running the business. Instead of spending all my time playing with dolls, I routinely practiced typing, taking notes, and touring my dad's office, particularly the computer room, which housed some of the nation's first mainframe computers.

My first business venture was selling my version of Girl Scout cookies. I wasn't old enough to be a Girl Scout, but I had watched my older sister sell the confections, and my mother was Girl Scout cookie chairman many times ... so why not?

I built my own Girl Scout cookie order form and then went house to house in our neighborhood and sold product. I came back and gave it to my mother and said, "Look what I did—you know, the Girl Scout thing." I didn't realize it at the time, but my mother had to bake all the cookies and box up all the orders, and then I delivered them to my customers. She never scolded me for doing this (even though *she* had to do all the work). Instead, she embraced my business "ingenuity" and supported my new venture. Both my parents gave me the foundation to step out into the world of "What ifs?"

My all-time favorite movie is *Forrest Gump*. I resonate with his character because his thought life and approach to life were so pure. He was a risk taker and faced and overcame adversity—recognizing adversity is key to knowing you are facing the unknown—without realizing what he was doing. And best of all, as he forged his path in life, he brought people along with him; life was never about him but about how he could make life better for others. To state the obvious, Forrest Gump wasn't in the top 2 percent academically. But, to me, he was in the top 2 percent of those who make the lives of others better. While he never asked the question "What if?" he took full advantage of the "gifts" life had given him, and he showed us what an extraordinary life can look like if we remain resilient and don't let limitations define us.

When I was fifteen, my parents had me complete an aptitude test that focused on my natural gifts. I secretly hoped my tests would reveal that I should continue developing my piano-playing skills and put Juilliard in my sights! But what I tested highest in was much more business focused. As I mentioned earlier, from a young age, business had been that thing that would light me up. I also learned that I had aptitudes in many different areas. This may be true for you as well. The problem is, if you don't express your aptitudes, or if you get pigeonholed into an area that doesn't allow you to express your true aptitudes, you will become frustrated with your life and you won't really understand why. I didn't want to be pigeonholed, which is what drove me to dig deeper and to find out that analytics and math and business fired me up. Giving people solutions to their problems … that lights me up.

We will go into more detail on this later in the book, but as you imagine your future career or rethink where you are in life and where you want to go, don't focus on the money—on how much you can make—focus on researching paths that align with your passion. Passion leads to purpose, and purpose is what you define yourself by. I can tell you from experience that the money will come, because passion and purpose will propel you, bringing you more career and life experiences, both of which are driving forces that will make you an in-demand person. A great example of this is Carly Fiorina, whom I deeply admire. She was part of the 98 percent club. In case you didn't know, Mrs. Fiorina

> … is an American businesswoman and politician, known primarily for her tenure as CEO of Hewlett-Packard (HP). As chief executive officer of HP from 1999 to 2005, Fiorina was the first woman to lead a Fortune Top-20 company. In 2002, Fiorina oversaw what was then the largest technology sector merger in history, in which HP acquired rival personal computer manufacturer, Compaq. The transaction made HP the world's largest seller of personal computers.[3]

But Carly didn't go to an Ivy League school, nor was she born with a "silver spoon." Her father was a professor and her mother an abstract painter. In 1980, she received a master of business administration, in marketing, from the Robert H. Smith School of Business at the University of Maryland, College Park, and in 1989 she graduated with a master of science degree in management from the MIT Sloan School of Management, under the Sloan Fellows program.[4]

This amazing woman grew up in what I call a "normal" family, and there is so much more to her incredible life and career, including her nonprofit work and her own charity, the Fiorina Foundation. The common thread to all she has accomplished is that she has been bold enough, and brave enough, to follow her passion and what lights her up.

At this point you might be thinking, *There are so many things that light me up. How do I know what path to follow? I don't want to jump around and never accomplish anything.*

Thanks to a wonderful pastor I met while living in Houston some years ago, I learned the gift and value of discernment. "Discernment is the ability to perceive, understand, and judge things clearly, especially those that are not obvious or straightforward."[5] Take time to understand your natural gifts, talents, and passions. Consider seeking out a trusted resource who is willing to listen to you and help you explore your passions so that you can begin to see a vision of what you want to do and where you want to go. The following websites and reading materials are great places for you to identify what lights you up and match it with how you have been innately created:

- The Highlands Ability Battery (HAB) "is a human assessment tool that objectively measures your natural abilities by asking you to perform specific tasks or exercises. As part of the

Highlands Whole Person Model, the HAB is the foundation and starting point to identify the career best suited for you."[6]

- The Johnson O'Connor Research Foundation offers an excellent assessment on understanding your aptitudes that "are natural talents or abilities, which predict the potential to do, or learn to do, certain kinds of tasks quickly and easily."[7]

- The 16 Personalities website offers an in-depth Meyers-Briggs assessment where "you'll learn what really drives, inspires, and worries different personality types, helping you build more meaningful relationships."[8]

- Gallup's CliftonStrengths online assessment helps you to "discover what you naturally do best; learn how to develop your greatest talents into strengths; use your personalized results and reports to maximize your potential."[9]

- I also highly recommend reading *What Color Is Your Parachute?* by Richard Bolles.

Building the Right Network

No matter where you find yourself on your career path, one of the keys to your success will be the network of relationships you build. As I wrote in the introduction, I cannot stress this enough.

From the day you graduate from school through to your third career stage, you will meet hundreds, if not thousands, of people.[10] Treasure them, and maintain contact with as many people as possible. This will build your network, which is one of the most important aspects of your career and life. Today, this is so easy to do! I regret I didn't do this early in my career, but I have learned the value of this precious asset, and I can tell you unequivocally that my network relationships are one of the most valuable aspects of everything I've done.

Your network is the place where you can give and receive—notice the order—which is advice I wish I had been given. So, I encourage you to never miss a contact. From day one, you have the opportunity to build a network of lifelong relationships!

To be honest, in the past I had a tendency to say goodbye and keep moving forward, not often looking back. I now realize that I left too many people behind. I will also tell you that I probably left certain roles too early, and those roles probably would have benefited me to a greater degree had I focused and relaxed into what I was doing *in the moment* and with whom I was blessed to do it instead of skipping ahead to the "What's next?" I should have let the fruit on the tree ripen just a little bit more.

But I was anxious; I was restless. I wanted to grab every ring that was put in front of me, and a lot of rings will be put in front of you. I should have let some of that career fruit mature a little bit more. And in later parts of my career, I learned to do just that. But in the beginning, I was off to the races, and every time somebody asked me about a potential new position, I was anxious to say yes. Sometimes I should have said, "Not yet." To be honest, if I had tapped into my network of relationships, I'm sure that someone would have given me the same advice, perhaps in words like "Slow down and take a good look at what you want to do before you do it."

My advice to you is this: You've got to keep those doors open. You've got to nurture those contacts. You've got to respect how others have poured into you. Yes, you will continually move on to something else, but moving on doesn't mean the end of any relationship. There are dozens of people I wish I had stayed in closer contact with, and I've learned that as I've grown.

I Didn't Do It Alone ... Nor Should You

As I reflect back on my career, I credit and have gratitude toward many people who took the time to weave their hands together and say, "Step here."

My first career role was as a life insurance salesperson at Mutual of New York, mainly because life insurance was my family's business. I loved math and had a talent for analytics and a passion for helping people. So, this was a logical fit for me. My family was the first group of individuals that wove their hands together to help me; in other words, they were the start of my network building. And I accepted their helping hand and extended my help to others. At the end of the day, life insurance is about protecting people from life's events, and I saw that as an honored position. With that mindset, I learned to be an individual producer, helping people attain their life goals, which also helped me become a successful life insurance salesperson. This role taught me so much about people, business, and providing solutions.

I could have stayed in this career position, grown my business, and led a very happy, fulfilling life. However, I am a risk taker and a bit of an explorer, looking for the new, new. So, a few years into this successful career rung, I switched industries and became a wholesale manufacturer's rep for three furniture companies. The role was totally different, in a totally different part of the country, and well beyond my own comfort zone. But there was still the thread of helping people and businesses with solutions.

In the early going, there were very lonely times, lots of tears, and many days of missing what I was comfortable with. But in the quiet of my reflections, I knew this time and taste of newness was something I would repeat over and over again if I was going to keep moving my career forward. Ultimately, I found my groove, and I also found an incredible mentor, Damon Casemore, with whom I am friends today. He had a family business, and working with him showed me how my role as a manufacturer's rep could help support the success of his business and the families it fed. My friend was, and continues to be, a major part of my network, and our relationship from the very beginning was another learning curve for me to maintain a "giving back" mindset.

• • • • •

I want to take a short segue and address the loneliness aspect of moving forward in your career. No matter how big your network may become, there are times when you will feel alone. The reason is this: others can walk your path *with* you, but no one can walk your path *for* you. If you want to grow, if you want to succeed in reaching your potential, then I encourage you to incorporate this mantra into your life: get comfortable with the uncomfortable.

Loneliness is only temporary. It can be a great teaching tool if you work hard to make your new relationships, to cultivate your new friends in the business, to find your new success points, and to always find ways to give back.

• • • • •

After a couple of years as a successful furniture representative, I felt it was time to move closer to home. The next move would be one that changed my life forever. I called on my network and soon found a company, AT&T, for which I could work not *in* my hometown but closer and in a much bigger city. I believe I was offered this great new position with AT&T because I had a demonstrated success record, and AT&T was looking for a new account advisor. This role once again took me into an industry I had never been in before: technology—specifically telecommunications.

Fortunately, the company's leadership saw me as someone who had learned how to uncover customer needs and provide appropriate solutions. They realized I had the basics of how to help people understand that they might have a gap in their business plan and that I could fill it with a particular product or service. Once again, I had to get comfortable with the uncomfortable.

One of the greatest blessings that came about during this time in my life was something that I truly believe was due to divine intervention. About the same time I joined AT&T, my future husband, Jim Tye, was going to work for AT&T in Orlando, Florida. I was in Jacksonville, and within a year he also transferred to Jacksonville, where we met. Thirty-three years later, we are still happily married. Thank you, AT&T!

You Can Do It!

If you are entering the workforce for the first time or are reentering after taking some time off, you may be wondering, *What do I have to offer? How can I take my skills and help a business, nonprofit, or others succeed?* These are great questions!

To begin with, you already have a network of people. If you are just entering the workforce, you may still have prior job roles, former professors and teachers, and, of course, family and friends. If you are reentering the workforce, you have all the people you've connected with in prior roles. Now, make a list, and reestablish contact with those people.

For those reentering the workforce, one special contact you should work to make is with those you know on the human resources side of your former (or future) companies. Let them know when you are changing jobs or careers, because they have a vision of all the talents that are needed within their organization, and you want them to remember your talent. And don't discount a simple message of "Can we have coffee?" "Is there anything I can help you with?" as well as "Is there anybody that could benefit from what I'm experienced in? I'm happy to talk to that person." Always make it a *give* before you *get*.

For those of you who have made it to the third stage—you've decided to retire and "retread"—take some time to deeply ponder what you've loved most about your career. What really lifted you up? What did a great day feel like? Then take the time to throw off the bow lines and consider the world of options before you. You have gifts, the time, and the talents, and the world has enormous needs. At this point, you may be able to enjoy becoming part of the "gig" economy or work only a few hours a week. But do what lights you up, and do it for as long as you can!

If you focus on what you can give and not only what you need or can get, you'll find that a universal principle will become a reality in your life: when you give, you will receive.[11]

• • • • •

I'm a big fan of the book *The First 90 Days*, by Michael D. Watkins. The book is a great testament to giving first and receiving second. Watkins writes that what makes a leader successful starts with learning what will make their own leader successful and how to contribute to that leader's success.[12]

Time and time again in my career, if I focused on how my leader would succeed, I would also soar forward from a success perspective. Obviously, all the leaders you have or have had should be a big part of your network. It's never too early—or too late—to have a mentor, somebody who is experienced and can be an invaluable network connection.

As a seasoned professional today, I still have mentors—people I trust with big decisions or difficult work issues. And I'm also a mentor for many, many folks in their early and midcareer stages. Don't do it alone; give back to move forward. Keep building your network. Yes, this is going to take work. You need to be diligent; you must document, and then you need to nurture your network. You need to find your rhythm of staying in touch with them and staying front of their mind. But never forget that networks are about relationships, and the best long-term relationships are win-win. Don't reach out only when you need something; reach out to offer help, a cup of coffee, a kind word, an encouraging email, or with a phone call saying, "Hi, I just wanted you to know that I was thinking about you, and I appreciate that you are part of my life."

YOU'RE THE ONE TO WEAVE YOUR HANDS TOGETHER AND SAY, "STEP HERE"

If you're a seasoned professional, you're likely at that beautiful place where you can truly make the choice to be the helping hand that someone else needs. You've succeeded in your thirty-plus-year career, and you know you have much more to give. But you don't want to step back into the all-consuming life of the ten-plus-hours-a-day work world.

Giving back in these ways is very fulfilling! In the words of the immortal Martin Luther King Jr., "Life's most persistent and urgent question is, 'What are you doing for others?'"[13]

If you think about it, none of us would be where we are today without at least one (and more likely several) people weaving their hands together and saying, "Step here." We all need others to give us a helping hand. Take a few moments to reflect on the sacrifices made by your parents, spouse, or partner. Consider the encouragement and generosity you've received from colleagues, teachers, and leaders. The successes we have achieved can be credited in large part because someone else took time to help, inspire, and/or challenge us. Now, ask yourself, *Where would I be if the people in my life had not given back in some way?*

As someone in the third stage of her career, one of the ways I enjoy giving back is through consulting and board work. Both of these "occupations" allow me to provide advice and counsel and allow others to take advantage of my years of experience with various business models and areas of leadership. I learned at an early age that "you give back to go forward."

Taking Care of Yourself

You can be brave, confident, and focused. But in order to do so, it's important to understand the value of *self-care*. As author and speaker Michael Hyatt's states, "You can't take care of anyone else unless you first take care of yourself."[14] Self-care isn't about being selfish, and it isn't about ego. Self-care puts you in a healthy position, emotionally and physically, so that you can move toward accomplishing your life and career goals. For me, daily early morning exercise is key to the success of my day. It gets my blood and brain pumping, clears the cobwebs, and gives me a fresh view of the day ahead. And after accomplishing a tough workout first thing in the morning, the rest of the day can look pretty easy!

Self-care can look different every day:

- Understanding how to set and reorganize priorities using a simple tool such as the Eisenhower Matrix:

The Eisenhower Matrix

	URGENT	NOT URGENT
IMPORTANT	Do: Tasks with deadlines or consequences.	Schedule: Tasks with unclear deadlines that contribute to long-term success.
NOT IMPORTANT	Delegate: Tasks that must get done but don't require your specific skill set.	Delete: Distractions and unnecessary tasks.

Team Asana, "Be Productive at Home: 11 Tips to Promote Efficiency [2023] • Asana," Asana, October 4, 2022, https://asana.com/resources/eisenhower-matrix.

- Treating your health as a top priority; without it, you won't actualize the life you deserve.

- Learning when to say yes and when to say no (setting boundaries).

- Resting—taking a breath, a vacation, or whatever type of release you need to reenergize.

- Investing in your family and your faith; they will both be there when you need them if you invest and nurture both.

The things you can do for self-care are endless, and they are unique to you! But the common denominator to all self-care involves *intentionality* and *mindfulness* to what you want to do. There are days you will celebrate and days you will struggle, and I encourage you to embrace what each day brings. Creating the discipline of self-care leads to heightened awareness as you build your emotional and mental capacity for your present and future needs. This is called "interoceptive awareness."[15]

Today's world of instant gratification and treat-yourself commercialized ideas of self-care "because I deserve this" doesn't allow room for us to slow down enough to listen to what we truly need. So, start your self-care journey by taking some time to figure out what you *really* need—body, soul, and spirit. Then take the necessary steps to start your self-care journey. That journey may take you in different directions, but it will last your entire lifetime.

A BIG WORD OF CAUTION

There are times in your self-care journey when you will "hit the wall." Hitting the wall means that you suddenly reach a mental block or impasse. This could be as simple as running out of ideas or as complex as not knowing what to do next in your life or career.

When I have hit that wall from a career perspective, I learned that it is not always the best to just push through. Instead, I've learned to pull out my résumé and use my gift of discernment. I ask myself questions such as *Why am I in this position? Why am I stuck right now? What can I learn from this time in my life? What is missing right now (i.e., one of those aptitudes)? Why do I feel out of sorts at this stage?*

Sometimes I've found that I've made a bad choice, and I need to face that, take responsibility, and then determine a different path. There have been times when I've written out my career steps to see how I've arrived in my current state and have asked myself why this particular one feels so bad right now. *Is my current place incongruent with who I am, my mission, and/or my skill set?*

Whenever you find yourself hitting the wall, no matter how busy you *think* you are, you will always feel trapped until you determine the source of your wall so you can then determine how best to move forward.

It Comes Down to Trust

I have talked about a lot of different topics in this chapter. I've also underscored the importance of relationships as the cornerstone of any success you may have. Now, I want to focus on the foundation of any and all relationships: trust.

According to the *Oxford English Dictionary*, the word *trust* means having a "firm belief in the reliability, truth, ability, or strength of someone or something."

To state the obvious, no matter what stage of your career you're in, I encourage you to bring with you an atmosphere of trust, because all successful organizations and teams are built on relationships, and relationships are built on trust.

Trust comes with credibility, and without credibility your voice will not be heard. Trust also comes with transparency about your intentions and your endgame. From watching some tough debates at the boardroom table over the years, I learned to use the phrase, "You and I are aligned on this." It is a great way to say, "Let's acknowledge common ground, which allows us to trust each other on at least part of an issue." Without some level of trust, your ability to bring others along will be very slow going, if it is going at all.

HOW IMPORTANT IS TRUST IN BUSINESS?

Author and speaker Stephen Covey has created an entire business based on the concept of "moving at the speed of trust." In a Forbes interview with Rodger D. Duncan, Covey notes the following:

> Trust always affects two measurable outcomes: speed and cost. When trust goes down—in a relationship, on a team, in a company, in an industry, with a customer—speed decreases with it. Everything takes longer. Simultaneously, costs increase. Redundancy processes, with everyone checking up on everyone else, cost more. In relationships, on teams, in companies, that's a tax. I call it a low-trust tax where literally everything is being taxed off the top. Where trust is low, everything takes longer and costs more.
>
> The opposite is true as well. When trust goes up in a relationship, or on a team, in a company, in an industry, with a client, with a customer—speed goes up with it and cost comes down. Everything happens faster and everything costs less because trust has been established. That's a dividend, a high-trust dividend. It's really that simple, that real, that predictable.[16]

Business strategist David Horsager speaks internationally on the bottom-line impact of trust. He has developed a system with which he teaches leaders how to build the "Eight Pillars of Trust":[17]

- Clarity—People trust the clear and mistrust the ambiguous.

- Compassion—People put faith in those who care beyond themselves.

- Character—People notice those who do what is right over what is easy.

- Competency—People have confidence in those who stay fresh, relevant, and capable.

- Commitment—People believe in those who stand through adversity.

- Connection—People want to follow, buy from, and be around friends.

- Contribution—People immediately respond to results.

- Consistency—People love to see the little things done consistently.

TRUST-BASED NETWORKING

Without trust, there can be no relationship on any level—personal or in business.

If you want to truly build a trust-based network, then make it your primary goal to help others develop their careers and businesses and achieve their goals. The purpose of trust-based networking is to help others. It goes beyond a transaction-based relationship of reciprocal favors and mutually beneficial obligations.

Granted, you cannot devote 100 percent of your time to helping others succeed, but if you reach out to others to build relationships—"Hey, I was thinking of you; would you like to grab a coffee or lunch and tell me what's going on in your life?" Or "You popped into my mind, so I thought I'd send you a 'Hi, how are you doing?' email"—you are building a trust-based network.

Always remember that when you are networking with trust, you are also leading with trust. And trust reciprocates trust.

Conclusion

You can have an extraordinary career! Be intentional about your networks, your skills and passions, and your future, even if it is the great unknown right now. No matter how digital the world becomes, success will always be relational and connectional, first and foremost. No one can do life alone—neither the 2 percenters nor the rest of us 98 percenters—so stay connected. Don't lose focus on what lights you up, and don't let go of your career connections. Staying in touch and building relationships and networks that are built on trust are so much easier in today's world. Make it a habit to routinely send an email or connect via social media. Your ability to reach out and touch someone is only limited by your imagination.

For those who have woven their hands together to help you, let them know how appreciative you are—especially if it has been a period of time since you last connected. If you focus on nurturing relationships—not for what you can get but for what you can give—the old saying, "What goes around comes around" will be evident in your network *and* your business success!

Finally, *never* neglect yourself. The common denominator in your network and relationships is y-o-u. Your well-being—spiritual, emotional, mental, and physical—is the cornerstone upon which your life and career is built. If you want to optimize all that you're doing, then you must prioritize your self-care.

Pattie Dale's Pertinent Points

- Know yourself! What are your talents, skills, and moments of life that bring you joy? How do those manifest themselves in your work world? And if they don't, how can you alter your current situation to make sure they do?

- Be aware of how important the people in your life are to you—not just now but for years and years to come. Build your network; nurture your network; trust your network.

- Be the person others want to keep in *their* network. When asked to, provide/advise/remind others to take care of themselves in specific ways.

- Be the trusted friend/ally/colleague for others that you want them to be for you!

CHAPTER 2

Everything Ladders Up

If you are going to climb the ladder of
success, first hold it for someone else.
—GERALD BROOKS

The term *ladder up* is relatively new to the twenty-first-century workplace. It is a modern twist on the more familiar term *climb the career ladder*. However, while climbing the ladder is something you do for yourself—for example, promotions that will help build your career—what I've experienced is that climbing the ladder involves *helping others* as you move up your career ladder. When you *ladder up*, it means that everything builds on everything else; nothing should be done in isolation or for exclusively your benefit but should connect or bolt onto something else—just like LEGO toys! Nothing should ever be wasted.

I also like to incorporate the term *twofer*; everything should have at least two uses, meaning it benefits both parties and creates a win-win. For example, if you are going to engage in community activities or giving back, there is nothing wrong in knowing which organizations would not only benefit from your talents and treasures but would also benefit you in meeting people and organizations that open doors for you from a career perspective.

Laddering up is similar to networking. Everyone you meet is a potential "rung" on your ladder to move you higher and wider in your career. You are also a rung on someone else's ladder as they move up in their career. This is really about your skills and experiences along with your network. For example, with my skills as an individual producer, I started helping people with gaps in their businesses or lives. I learned to take those skills and deploy them to my team as a first-time team leader. This position developed my skills further, which led to the next rung on my career ladder—and also helped me to be a rung on someone else's ladder. That is what laddering up is all about!

As I look back on my work life, I can see the metaphorical ladder I've climbed, and in my mind, I can see the "rungs"—the people—who have helped me. When I was in senior management at Humana, I made it my goal to help others ladder up. I would take the time to meet individuals and find out what their career goals were, then I would do whatever I could to help them move up their own ladder. One of the great leaders I had the good fortune to work with was Tony Chase. He taught me the value of "lifting" while you climb. Tony never turned down a meeting request; he was the best at helping others make the move to their best place in life. I always try to do the same, and I also ask those I help to pay it forward, to help someone else.

There is a third meaning to the phrase *ladder up*: everything has a common thread. You may look at your current career position and what may look like a jumble of disparate parts—promotions, career moves, etc.—that are seemingly disconnected. However, if you take the time to look into the details, you're likely to find a common thread that has woven, and continues to weave, itself together. The strongest fiber in the thread should be those skills, gifts, and talents that light you up. Over years and decades of your career, you'll express them in a myriad of different opportunities and roles, helping that thread become much stronger and more visible. You'll become known for certain of those great skills and gifts. You'll be sought out when there is a need for exactly the gifts and skills you possess, over and over again. So, stay focused on those light-me-up skills and talents that you possess!

You Can't Rush

No matter what career stage you are in—starting out, reentering the workforce, or looking for ways to give back as a seasoned professional—your career journey is, and always will be, a vital part of your life. Just like you can't run up and down a physical ladder, you cannot "run" through your professional path.

As I look back on my career, I can point to some missteps I've taken—the wrong promotion and/or company at the wrong time—and these have happened because I didn't think through what I was about to do, nor did I consult my network or mentors ... I just jumped!

One particular wrong jump was following a former leader into a small start-up company. It didn't take long for me to see that our values didn't align, our cultures were entirely different, and I was never going to be comfortable or passionate about this big leadership role. I will tell you there were tears and much, much loneliness. But I will also tell you that I do what I often do when I am in the lonely trough—I prayed for guidance and forgiveness. And soon enough, the phone rang! From that point on, I never lost sight of the lesson of making sure my values and cultures don't clash with those of the company I am considering joining.

Your career can't be rushed! Yes, there are times when you'll have to make a snap decision, but these are rare, and you'll usually have time to consider your next step. As the old saying succinctly goes, "It's a marathon, not a sprint," so settle in for the long haul. You will have many amazing experiences, and you will learn and grow a lot! Eventually, you'll see the bright, strong thread that weaves together those experiences and all that you have learned. And you'll see those rungs on the ladder, and also those who helped you to climb!

One beautiful part of your career will be those people you will meet along the way who will see that thread before you can. Those important actors in your life will pick you up and put you on a path you never saw coming, but later, their actions will make total sense to you, and you'll see that everything does ladder up! Trust them, and treasure them.

For me, one of those people was Jim Murray, whom I met when he was Humana's chief operating officer. Jim took a risk bringing me into Humana, which was an incredible career experience for me. He scooped me up when I wasn't even in the healthcare industry and didn't know how to spell *deductible*. But he had the discernment to know I had what it took to lead Humana's important and difficult market—Houston, Texas.

Jim looked and saw the rungs and threads in my life that made him believe in my skills. I'll never forget him saying, "This is a leader we want to have." I would never have self-selected myself for the role. It took someone else seeing the patterns in my life, my talent, and my career to see where I could go.

Laddering Up in Action

In chapter 1, I briefly mentioned some of my early jobs. You might be wondering how I went from furniture and insurance to the role of president at Humana. Here is part of my "laddering up" career journey.

Using those skills and gifts (my "light-me-ups") of analytics and solving for win-win solutions, my first roles were as an individual producer (insurance sales and furniture sales). Success in those two companies caught the eye of AT&T, and a person in my network made a valuable introduction for me.

My initial role at AT&T was to increase top-line revenues for this multinational company. During a very successful eleven-year career there, I won national sales awards, was placed on the Leadership Continuity Program (top 2 percent of the company), and honed my skills as a business and people leader. I learned what "building my brand" meant; I learned how to make sure my leader succeeded before I did, and I learned the value of a large, well-nurtured network. Those skills laddered up to help me move out of the big and beautiful corporate world of AT&T into the riskier world of a start-up firm.

Over the next seven years, I expanded my expertise in business operations, becoming the chief operating officer for two large customer contact businesses. This oversight allowed me to understand and operate more strategically in optimizing and accelerating top- and bottom-line revenue. From initial start-up to twenty-four months later, one of the firms I helped lead moved to a positive position in terms of earnings before interest, taxes, depreciation, and amortization (EBITDA) and, ultimately, was successfully positioned for acquisition in its sixth year of operation. These experiences were *all* new to me; I had no idea how to impact EBITDA when I entered this world. But again, there were people who saw in me things I didn't see myself; they wove their hands together and said, "Step here." Those invaluable seven years set me up for the most important career change in my life: moving back into the big and beautiful corporate world, but this time into the ever-exciting and changing world of healthcare—into Humana.

During my thirteen years at Humana, I held executive leadership roles across different markets and different business segments, learning and building my skills and network all along the way. Initially, Humana's COO, Jim Murray, and Bill Tait, Humana's senior vice president of markets, brought me on as president of Humana's Houston Health Plan to turn the plan to profitability. Within thirty-six months, I identified deficiencies in the current model, reduced the cost of goods sold, realigned the distribution model, and built a strong brand presence in the market. This time in my career showed me that "doing good by doing well" was possible and that it aligned with my belief that giving back to move forward should be at the core of any business success.[18] Humana became known as a true community partner in Houston for the first time. The business benefited while the community also benefited. This illustrated another of my core beliefs: generosity in life is foundational to success in life.

When Humana elevated me to president of the Humana Large Employer Segment in 2012, holding me accountable for $3 billion in top-line premium revenues, there was an expectation to turn this segment to profitability. Using a strategy that focused efforts on the account size and product type, which would yield a stronger return on invested capital, the segment ultimately turned to profitability.

In 2014, Humana's board of directors charged the CEO and COO with optimizing and fortifying the company's most profitable revenue stream, Medicare markets. I was asked to lead a strategic shift in Humana's sustainable/profitable growth approach, which became Humana's "Bold Goal." This work required redrafting how we treated all Humana patients and members. No longer could we assume that eight hours per year in a physician's office would offer sustainable health improvement.

This was a significant shift, because the company was moving from a simple "transaction" point of view to one of developing and caring about relationships. The company set about doing what was needed to help these people improve their health inside and outside their physician's office. We took a deeper approach to understanding our patients' lives and what barriers and social determinants of health prevented them from seeing the full results of their physician's treatment plans. We organized the many available community-based health programs, making them more accessible to members and patients. This work formed Humana's population health strategy and has elevated Humana as an industry leader in community and population health. And for me, it was the *perfect* combination of doing good while doing well, of seeing a business truly invest in solutions for those in need. A true "happy dance" moment!

• • • • •

I'm now in the third stage of my career as a private board director, business consultant, and Forbes author, and I continue to ladder up. I'm growing as a person and as a professional, and I'm finding new ways to be rungs on the ladders of others. And I love my work! More than thirty years ago, I was someone starting out, perhaps just like you. Years later, I became the person helping to create change in the social fabric of communities in the United States. Now, as a seasoned professional, I want to be someone who helps improve the lives of those on their career journey—to help others see the strong threads throughout their career that weave it all together. I want to help others find their light-me-up talents and use them to their fullest. I want to continue to help businesses refine their models for ultimate success. And I get to continue to earn money because it feeds my innate need to give back and to be a generous contributor to the social fabric of my community and the world.

Everything ladders up!

ering applying for a new role or a role at a different company. u don't know if you have the skills or experience for the new role. u can't let the unknown stop you (and in many, many aspects of , you never consider letting the unknown stop you). In the work rld, you'll need to accept the fact that discomfort in the new is part the process. You'll need to learn to "get comfortable with being comfortable."

I describe those periods of newness in a role as akin to being the back of a horse that you have not ridden before. As you go und the corral, that horse is going to test you. Sometimes it's going hrow you off. It's going to bang you into the side of the corral at es. But if you keep riding, if you keep trusting, then before you w it, you and the horse are in sync as you move together around corral. As confidence and familiarity build, the speed will come

If you think about it, being uncomfortable in something new ood for us because it's the starting point in order to grow and n. For example, if you want to get in better physical shape, you'll d to change your diet and start exercising, both of which will be omfortable in the beginning. I have run over twenty marathons, every single one started out feeling very uncomfortable in the nning. But I knew my body and my breathing would ultimately e into sync, and my running would be much more comfortable. u want to learn a new work-related skill, you have to sign up for nline program or perhaps seek out formal education; both may be mfortable at the beginning because of the "new" you are facing. ct, anything you want to do to improve your life or your career s with "getting comfortable with the uncomfortable."

Over your thirty-, forty-, or fifty-year career, you will experience tless things that are new. You will experience new teams, new

> ## Pattie Dale's Pertinent Points
>
> - When you "ladder up," it means that everything builds on everything else; nothing should be done in isolation or for exclusively your benefit but should connect like a LEGO tower.
> - Everyone you meet is a potential rung on your ladder to move you higher and higher in your vocation. You are also a rung on someone else's ladder as they move up in their career.
> - Your career can't be rushed! Yes, there are times when you'll have to make a snap decision, but these are rare, and you'll usually have time to consider your next step.

CHAPTER 3

The Discomfor
of the New

You pushed me into many new career mov
careful to architect those new moves in a
"laddered" up and gave me an exception
—DEDICATED TO MY LEADERS A
LARRY BELL, BILL TYNDAL, NOR

Throughout my career, I've learned to
mantra: get comfortable being unco
you read those words, you might be th
you crazy? Those who agree with the
risk takers by nature; those who don't agree tend
vative and risk averse in their outlook. Neither si
is wrong: risk takers can easily take a wrong path
always think things through; those who are mo
miss out on opportunities because they are slow i

Anything new often brings with it a level of
we don't know what the unknown holds. For e

roles, new leaders, new strategies, new office spaces, new technology, new policies, and on and on and on.

Here is a key to embracing understanding the discomfort of the new: you'll go through a learning curve, which shows that the first part of the new often leads to less efficiency until the new fades and is replaced by the knowledge of what your role entails.

The time spent *learning* rather than *doing* can feel uncomfortable, and it can also be quite intimidating. However, you must realize that the discomfort of the new will happen countless times over your career. Anxiety arises because of the discomfort of the new. Procrastination happens because of the discomfort of the new. Avoidance happens because of the discomfort of the new. The discomfort of the new can also cause you to miss out on new opportunities, new roles, and new career changes. However, when you learn to accept the discomfort of the new, you may not enjoy how you feel in the moment, but you can remind yourself that something good, or even big, is about to happen. You are going to learn new skills, meet new people, and experience new business and working models.

During my career at AT&T, I was fortunate to have exceptional mentors and supporters. These leaders encouraged me to take on new roles, many of which required relocating to a new AT&T location. With each new role, I was able to learn and grow and develop. And just when I got comfortable, *poof!*—it was time to move again. These leaders had traveled the path before me and could see in me things I did not see in myself, but I trusted them with my career, and that trust paid off enormously. The experiences I enjoyed at AT&T gave me the solid brand, confidence, and foundation I needed to learn that stepping into a new and challenging role is one of the most important "skills" you can learn in your career.

The Learning Curve

Accepting the discomfort of the new is the entry point to any new role, position, or career change. It is also the starting point of what is called the "learning curve." *Collins English Dictionary* notes that "a learning curve is a process where people develop a skill by learning from their mistakes."[19] I would add that wise people know that a learning curve includes learning from the mistakes of others and mistakes of your own.

I once heard a speaker describe a learning curve this way:

1. You don't know what you don't know.

2. You know what you don't know.

3. You learn everything you can about what you don't know.

4. What you didn't know is now what you know and can do.

In his book *Outliers*, author Malcolm Gladwell notes that "the closer psychologists look at the careers of the gifted, the smaller the role innate talent seems to play and the bigger the role preparation seems to play."[20] What a brilliant statement for all of us in the 98 percent to remember! Every day, you can prepare for what is ahead. Before you know it, you turn around, and your first thirty days are behind you, then sixty and ninety days. You are starting to get your "operational legs" underneath you, and you can say, "I've done something that gives my leadership credibility that they've hired the right person."

After six months, you've done things that have added value and have helped your team—whether direct reports or those you work for—blossom and bloom. After a year, you've tackled it all, and you have full ownership. You also have education and experience that you can take with you to your next position or career move as you ladder up. And you'll be able to look back at the "discomfort of new" and know you have an end point, and you can affirm anything new is going to be uncomfortable until it's not. You are now comfortable with being uncomfortable. After all, in life, if we are lucky, every day will bring something new that we might be uncomfortable with! Or, as Eleanor Roosevelt said, "Do one thing every day that scares you."

What Lights You Up?

One of the first, and most important, things I do when taking on a new role or new assignment is to be intentional in remembering those skills, talents, and areas of life that light me up. And then I track that (let it ladder up!) to understand *why* this position lights me up!

Why am I the right person at the right time for the business, company, not-for-profit? *Why* is this role important to those I will report to or lead? And *why* is this role important to the end user in the grand scheme of things?

You'll want to ask yourself those same questions. Determining what lights you up—your "why"—will give you the passion and purpose to get you through the mundane moments as well as the highs and lows that inevitably come with any role you occupy.

Asking why came into vogue in the last decade through Simon Sinek. Samuel Thomas Davis summarizes Sinek's book *Start with Why: How Great Leaders Inspire Everyone to Take Action* by explaining as follows:[21]

The Book in Three Sentences

1. The ability to inspire those around you and to achieve remarkable things starts with WHY.

2. Any organization can explain what it does; some can explain how they do it; but very few can clearly articulate why.

3. Those who start with WHY never manipulate, they inspire.

The Five Big Ideas

1. Your WHY is your purpose, cause or belief.

2. Every inspiring leader and organization, regardless of size or industry, starts with WHY.

3. People don't buy WHAT you do, they buy WHY you do it.

4. Knowing our WHY is essential for lasting success and the ability to avoid being lumped in with others.[22]

5. When your WHY goes fuzzy, it becomes much more difficult to maintain the growth, loyalty, and inspiration that helped drive your original success.

When you take the time to understand *why* your new role matters and find out whom it matters to, you will set yourself up for success.

Your Ninety-Day Plan[23]

Michael Watkins, author of *The First 90 Days,* states, "The most important decisions you make in your first 90 days will probably be about people."[24] I love this book because it is a very detailed, step-by-step guide to helping you discern what you can do to make your role transition successful. By doing your own job really well, you enable others to succeed. That sparks the generosity flame in me and clears my path of the noise of the new, helping me focus on succeeding through my leaders' and teams' success.

In his book, Watkins gives seven tips to avoid the "transition trap" when moving into a new role.[25] Here is my summary:

- *Sticking to what you know*: You believe you will be successful in the new role by doing the same things you did in your previous role.

- *Falling prey to the "action imperative"*: You feel as if you need to take action, and you try too hard too early to put your own stamp on the organization.

- *Setting unrealistic expectations*: You don't negotiate your mandate or establish clear, achievable objections.

- *Attempting to do too much*: You rush off in all directions, launching multiple initiatives in the hope that some will pay off.

- *Coming in with "the" answer*: When you make a decision, you don't like to include others, because they may know more than you due to their experience. This causes you to squander opportunities, because you already have your mind made up or you jump to conclusions and/or premature solutions.

- *Engaging in the wrong type of learning*: Spending too much time on the "technical" side of the business means you miss out on learning about the culture and politics of your new role. You neglect to find out about cultural insights, relationships, and other information that can help you understand what is going on.

- *Neglecting horizontal relationships*: You spend too much time focused on vertical relationships and not enough on peers and other stakeholders.

As you envision your first ninety days in your new role, the obvious area of focus is on what *you* need to do, what tasks *you* need to accomplish, what path *you* need to take. But because you are in a new role, what you need to do, the tasks you need to accomplish, and the path you need to take is either unfamiliar or unknown. This may cause you endless stress and anxiety—I know, I've been in that position.

What I've learned was that my focus was on the wrong person. It should *not* have been on me but rather on those I was going to lead and be led by. What do these people need? What tasks are they seeking to accomplish? What path do they need to take? When you figure out the needs that others have, you can then crystalize your role—which is, first and foremost, to help those you lead, or are led by, succeed. After all, that is why you're in your current position. Your job mission then becomes helping others succeed by aligning your education, skills, and experiences with their goals and objectives so that together, you accomplish the overarching organizational goals and strategies.

How do you write out your own, unique ninety-day plan? Here are some tips:

1. Determine What You Need to Accomplish
   Within your first ninety days, there are big-picture goals you want to accomplish that might seem overwhelming at first. You have so many ideas swirling around in your head that you may not know where you want to start. So, start by taking each goal and breaking it into smaller, more detailed assignments/roles/responsibilities over a ninety-, sixty-, and thirty-day time period. Notice that you start with the longer time frame so that your accomplished goals build on one another.

   Setting these goals starts with the reason you were hired in the first place: What does senior leadership expect of you? What, if any, objectives were set out for you? Does your team have specific goals it needs to accomplish within the next ninety days? What are your priorities and expectations? Answering big-picture questions like these will help you identify what you want—and need—to accomplish.

2. Make the Most of Every Meeting
   - Study the meeting agenda well in advance.
   - Do your research to understand how you can contribute to the outcome.
   - Have a premeeting with some of your colleagues to make sure you understand *why* you've been included in the meeting in the first place.

   Don't just occupy the seat. Own it! But do not overlook the fact that there is great power in listening both premeeting and during the meeting. Listening will ultimately pay you more dividends than constantly speaking, as long as when you do speak, the value of your contribution is strong, generous, and respectful.

3. Use a Goal-Setting Model
   You are ready to set your ninety-day goals, but you're unsure exactly how to do this. One reason might be that you are not sure what plan of action to take. The beauty of goal setting is that it's unique to you—your style, your personality—so you don't have to take a one-shoe-fits-all approach. To help you determine what goal-setting model might work for you, here is an overview of the most popular, time-tested models used throughout the business world:
   - *SMART Goals:* SMART stands for specific, measurable, achievable, relevant, and time-bound.

- *OKRs:* OKRs, or objectives and key results, align measurable outcomes that support overall business objectives.

- *GROW Goals:* This is an acronym for goal, reality, options, and way forward that focuses on having a clear goal as a starting point, evaluating the current reality, investigating options, and detailing the way forward.

- *Locke and Latham's Five Principles of Goal Setting:* Similar to SMART goals, this model focuses on setting goals that are specific, challenging, achievable, relevant, and time-bound.

- *Backward Goals:* Backward goals start with the end goal and work backward to identify the steps needed to complete the objective.[26]

- *Values-Based Goals:* This model is designed to align personal and professional goals with individual values and beliefs.

- *4DX:* The "Four Disciplines of Execution" is designed to improve execution and accountability by setting and achieving high-impact goals through a series of personal and/or business-related disciplines.[27]

4. Soak It Up

   Ask questions about the company, culture, goals, and challenges, and stay open minded. Find out about existing strategies, plans/goals to achieve, and what your predecessor achieved and where they fell short. Soak in as much information as you can. If there was no predecessor—lucky you … a newly created role!—find out what gaps existed that made this new role so valuable.

5. Build Relationships

   You will never succeed without developing trust-based relationships. You need to meet with as many people as possible to get their take and opinions and understand their viewpoints. Certainly you want to share your vision, ideas, and goals, but relationships are not built on "facts" but rather on intangibles such as rapport, personality, and communication style. Try to learn about an individual before meeting with them for the first time. LinkedIn may be a great resource.

6. Flexibility

   Keep in mind your ninety-day plan is not written in stone. It is a detailed guide for you that must be checked regularly and changed/adapted to the reality you'll be facing.

7. Don't Be a Lone Ranger

   Once you've completed your ninety-day plan, have someone else review it, ideally your leader and members of your team. Getting input from others will help you identify gaps and remedy them. Be wary of adding or changing too much; it's good to be flexible, but at the end of the day, the plan is yours to carry out.

PLANNING TO SUCCEED

I'm sure you've heard the saying, "If you fail to plan, you plan to fail." However, if you have a ninety-day plan in place going into your new position, you will be planning to succeed!

Having a ninety-day plan in place will give you clarity of purpose and direction as you set priorities to accomplish within a given time frame. It is a self-service guide, a valuable resource, and an I've-done-that checklist. You can identify the challenges ahead of you, the goals you want to achieve, whom you want to meet and when, and so much more. Best of all, you will have the confidence to move forward into the unknown.

• • • • •

After understanding what my team and leaders need to be successful, in addition to the ninety-day plan I develop a business plan for my new role. The fastest way to get a new position under control is to be intentional about how to accomplish the work to be done, and a business plan allows me to do that.

The first part of the plan is assessing the assets available to me. What are the tools in my toolbox? What are my team's talents and strengths? What is working, and what needs refreshing? And, again, what will my leader be judged on, and how might my team help bring about his/her success?

I also consider time frames—i.e., how much time do I need to spend in discovery? Every new role has a discovery phase in which you'll discover what you knew and were told as well as what you don't know and were not told. Learn everything you can about the new role. And find out what happened to the last person who was in this role. Did they succeed and go on to something bigger? Or did they fail at the role? It's important to understand both sides of that equation: How did they succeed? If they didn't, what caused them to fail? That's a really important part of your discovery time.

Never forget that the real reason you are hired for any position is to contribute to the success of others and the overall success of the organization. Determining exactly how and what you will contribute can be uncomfortable at first, and one of the ways you can make this a little less uncomfortable is by understanding the overall company strategy and its component parts.

Focus on what your leader or subordinates will be judged by, and then go about making sure you help that leader succeed. That will give you deeper knowledge and greater credibility and will give you opportunities to be "generous" to those you lead and who lead you. When you view your new role in this way, you are looking at it in the right way. Remember, you have to fully understand the organization's strategy to fully understand your role within that strategy. This must be the starting point for your first ninety days and for the business plan you establish to succeed in those first ninety days and beyond.

Make a Lasting Impression

An outstanding leader once told me, "The president of the United States is the only one who gets a hundred days to do something. You need to do something in the first ninety days." Since then, I have always wanted to *quickly* learn what makes the organization I lead or my leader's world go around and how to contribute to that success.

In your first ninety days, you must be brave, confident, and focused:

- Show up ready and prepared every day.

- Be on time.

- Try to be among the last ones to leave.

- Act, dress, and perform like a professional.

- Have a "continuously learning" mindset.

Incorporating these points into all you do will establish a habit and pattern that will follow well beyond day ninety-one. And you will *quickly* find that the uncomfortable is getting more and more comfortable!

RELATIONSHIPS

One of the easiest ways to build relationships with your leaders and coworkers in the first ninety days is by developing *trust*. We discovered the importance of trust in chapter 1, and I'd like to expand on the topic a little more.

You need to be the trusted source of whatever you're putting forth and have coworkers, leaders, customers, and clients count on your authenticity and truth. That doesn't happen without a lot of work and effort, but it's within your grasp and ability to do.

Refer back to your business plan:

- What are your team's, leader's, and organization's goals for this month, quarter, and year?

- What are their barriers to accomplishing those goals?

- What is your role in impacting and achieving those goals?

When you understand the first two points and then use the third one to accomplish both of them, you will establish trust—others will trust that you know what you're doing, and you will fulfill your role to bring about overall success.

Looking back at my time in the furniture business, I see that the owner and I built a relationship of mutual trust. I took the time to learn his business's language, metrics, and barriers to success, and he took the time to teach me. When I demonstrated to him how my small role could help push an obstacle out of the way or help him move closer to success, our professional relationship grew exponentially. He still helps me with business advice and decisions today, almost thirty years later! What started out as a very uncomfortable place for me—new city, new industry, new client base—ended up not only becoming a warm and comfortable place but gave me many new rungs on my ladder to be used for the next chapters in my life!

NO NEED TO BE THE SMARTEST—BE COMFORTABLE WITH THAT FACT!

I remember that when I took my first big role at AT&T headquarters, my father told me, "Always remember that in the beginning, you're not the smartest person at the table." As you move through your first ninety days, how you come across to others will establish your reputation. So, ask yourself, *What do I want my reputation to be?* When you sit down with your team, you are new, and they are not. They are wiser than you are, even if you were brought in to lead.

As a leader, during your first ninety days it takes a ton of self-discipline to acknowledge that you are not the smartest person in the room. It goes against our nature, and it is very uncomfortable. But there's a richness—a deeply satisfying level of humility—to letting go and letting your team tell you what you need to know in a generous, nonthreatening way.

When I started my new role as district manager at AT&T's headquarters, I was probably the least talkative person at the table for the first month. I was absorbing information, taking notes, and learning, all of which helped in refining my business plan and informing my future decision-making. I respected the knowledge of my team; this was new ground for me but not new ground for them. And my not having a know-it-all attitude was the foundation of our new trusting relationship, and it made all the difference in the world.

I took this lesson into my role as market president of Humana. I was not only a new leader but a new leader in a very established industry and market. I had team members who resisted my leadership because I was such a novice in their industry. I could feel the "What does she know? We've been doing this forever" atmosphere when I was first brought in to lead the team.

But I was hired for a reason, and I knew that winning over the team and establishing trust were a marathon, not a sprint. Even though I had resistant team members, I knew that if I would stay the course through humility and learning over the next ninety days, I would establish the necessary trust between us. I was cautioned ahead of time that this was a difficult team, and I knew we would all have to work hard to get to a healthy environment during that first ninety days.

Remember, your leaders and fellow team members will count on you and your help all along the way. That's why you were brought into the company—to help others succeed by succeeding yourself. Look at what your leader does for their leader. Understand how your team functions when they are at their best. Refine your business plan, and understand the why behind what's asked of you, your team, and your leadership. When all those component parts are succeeding, you will succeed as well; it all ladders up!

BUILDING YOUR BRAND

The old saying, "You never get a second chance to make a first impression" holds true during your first ninety days. During this time, you are building your "brand," or your reputation, so plan accordingly. When you are meeting someone for the first time, ask yourself, *What impression do I want this person to have of me?*

In an insightful LinkedIn article, Paul Petrone identifies six basic things that will establish, enhance, or repair someone's reputation:[28]

1. You show up to meetings on time.

   If you are less senior at your organization and you consistently show up late, people think you are flighty and don't know what you are doing. Conversely, if you are more senior at your organization and you consistently show up late, people think you are arrogant and don't care about them.

2. You make the most out of meetings.

   Meetings have such a bad rap. But they don't have to; meetings have the potential to be the most invigorating part of your day. To make that happen, you need to do a few things. As far as attending meetings, it means doing the prereads and coming prepared with questions. And it means not being on your phone or computer during the meeting but instead focusing on what's being said.

   As far as calling your own meetings, it means only calling meetings when they are absolutely necessary and ensuring that next steps are clear. This shows that you have your stuff together and you value other people's time. When I coach my team members about hosting meetings, I tell them that if they can't get their message across articulately and impactfully in twenty minutes or less, they don't have any business holding the meetings. Why twenty minutes? A mentor once told me that's the perfect length of time to ask others for. Whether it's an in-person meeting, over coffee, or on the phone, this is a minimal time commitment. It gives you a clear timeline to plan for and is an easier request for busy people to accept.

   You might think you have enough knowledge or skill to wing it in the meeting. But don't you dare when it's an important meeting and you want that person to remember your name! Show up prepared, even if you're not completely confident. This will show your capability and demonstrate your potential. Before I met with my mentor (or anyone), I practiced in front of the mirror, on the car ride over, and in my head before the meeting. I anticipated questions and practiced my answers. And you know what? I nailed it!

3. You take control of your own development.
   It's not your boss's job or your organization's job to develop you. They can offer the tools and feedback to help you develop yourself, but ultimately it's up to you to develop you.

4. You understand the strategy of your organization and tie your work into that.
   Your job is not on an island. Your job is to help your organization accomplish what it's seeking to accomplish, and your work varies depending on how your organization's strategy changes.

5. You are open to change instead of fighting it.
   This is an area where many professionals fall short. They constantly fight change, probably because we as humans are evolutionarily hardwired to resist it.

6. You treat people with respect and common courtesy.
   I think there's no more incorrect statement in business than "nice guys finish last." Being a generally nice person who treats other people with respect and courtesy is a massive competitive advantage in the workplace.

See Yourself at the End

In his legendary business book *7 Habits of Highly Successful People*, Stephen Covey's Habit 2 is "Begin with the End in Mind," which means to "define clear measures of success and a plan to achieve them."[29] In my vernacular, I would put it this way: As you look outside your office, what do you want to see at the end of your career? Where will you be, and what will the setting depict—an executive office in the middle of a bustling downtown; a work-at-home office with the sounds of your family coming through?

What does that view and that setting tell you about where you want to be and what you want to have achieved on that last day of your career? What this means is that you have to *envision* where you want to be. It has to be a reality in your mind before it will become a reality in your life.

My vision was to have my own beautiful office with a dedicated assistant just outside my door. This achievement meant that I had become an executive or corporate officer. I also envisioned working in a vibrant downtown, surrounded by company headquarters in the tallest buildings, because I saw corporate life as something very exciting.

Seven years later, I was promoted to lead Humana's National Large Business division. It meant a move to Humana's headquarters location, 500 West Main Street in Louisville, Kentucky. I recall gazing out my window at all the tall buildings around me, then I looked through my open office door, and there was my wonderful dedicated assistant. That was a happy dance moment! Envision it, then be intentional about building your plan to achieve it!

It's easy to focus on the beginning and the middle of your career. But will doing so get you where you want to go? Typically, you remain hyperfocused on your current rung, or perhaps two or three rungs, as you ladder up. But I'm advocating that no matter where you are in your career, take the opportunity to see yourself at the end. Doing so gives you a career "compass" to guide you along an unknown path that leads to a known destination. And you'll surely know when you've arrived!

Be the REAL You

One of the biggest challenges I've had to overcome in my career was learning to silence negative voices that aim to take away my confidence.

I'm sure you've heard of the term *impostor syndrome*. In describing this term, freelance writer Arlene Cuncic succinctly writes,[30]

> Impostor syndrome is the internal psychological experience of feeling like a phony in some area of your life, despite any success that you have achieved in that area.

> You might have imposter syndrome if you find yourself consistently experiencing self-doubt, even in areas where you typically excel. Imposter syndrome may feel like restlessness and nervousness, and it may manifest as negative self-talk. Symptoms of anxiety and depression often accompany imposter syndrome.

Impostor syndrome will show up when you least expect it. You've fully prepared for a job interview when the nagging doubts start to creep in. You know you nailed the job application process, then you wonder if you missed something. Or, you scan the job websites because you know you're ready to move on in your career ... until you see the qualifications for the positions you are seeking. Trust me when I say this: most people alive on planet Earth can identify with impostor syndrome. Why do I say that? Because imposter syndrome doesn't care about one's social status, work background, skill level, or degree of expertise.

Here are some impostor syndrome characteristics:[31]

- An inability to realistically assess your competence and skills

- Attributing your success to external factors

- Berating your performance

- Fear that you won't live up to expectations

- Sabotaging your own success

- Self-doubt

- Setting very challenging goals and feeling disappointed when you fall short

If we were honest with ourselves, we would all say that we've suffered from impostor syndrome. I certainly have, most often during the first ninety days of starting a new job or career. That's why we all need to remember that our careers are a marathon, not a sprint.

On many a dark day I've recalled one of my favorite scriptures, Jeremiah 29:11, which I will paraphrase: God knows the plans He has for you, plans to give you a hope and a future, and will prosper you. It has helped me reorder my thoughts and settle my mind.

You are here for a reason. You are in your current position for a reason. You are starting a new career for a reason. You are ready to give back for a reason. Yes, you are going to struggle some days. Yes, there are times you will say, "Am I doing the right thing?" It's not supposed to feel comfortable or successful every single day. But if you constantly remind yourself that you are here for a reason—and stay focused on that reason—you will be able to learn and grow in rough times, celebrate the good times and victories you achieve, and help others achieve.

When I received my first major promotion at Humana, I was a new executive leader in a role well above my comfort zone. Unfortunately, the industry underwent massive changes only a short time after my wonderful promotion. While I thought I'd done a fine job of leading, I had to give up my leadership and span of my control to another senior staff member. That rattled my confidence. It almost affirmed a nagging fear that I shouldn't have been there in the first place.[32]

Imposter syndrome started sitting on my shoulder, and I had to knock it down. I had to go back to the basics and remember *why* I was hired for this position. I had to acknowledge that none of the reasons had been invalidated and that circumstances had merely changed, not my value or worth. That career shift led to the career move of a lifetime, allowing me to exercise generosity deeply, lean into communities, and develop new young leaders who had strong passion for their work and the communities we served.

Experiences from setbacks and resulting imposter syndrome will happen during your career. Don't panic; you are not alone. *Forbes* notes that 82 percent of adults have experienced imposter syndrome.[33] But remember, you control the outcome—nobody else.

Keep telling yourself that you were chosen for a reason. You are really good at this role, business, or service, so get to work on the business of *that*. Take time to remember why you are there, listen and learn from others on your team or in your industry, and then apply your knowledge and keep "riding around that horse." Success will come, but as often as you need to, keep repeating, "I am here for a reason. I am not the great imposter!"

A WORD TO WOMEN

Statistics show that women struggle with impostor syndrome more than men. When a woman applies for a role or puts herself out there for a role, if there are one or two things in the job description that make her feel unworthy, she may self-select out. However, if a man sees several things listed that he doesn't currently have the skills for, he most often has the confidence to think, *I don't have the skills right now, but I can certainly learn them.*

In an article written for *Forbes* magazine, contributor Kathy Caprino interviewed Laura Newinski, KPMG's US deputy chair and COO, about a survey the company produced for a KPMG's Women's Leadership Summit. Of the 750 executive women surveyed from major companies the study found the following:[34]

- A decisive 75 percent of executive women identified having experienced imposter syndrome at various points during their careers—and 85 percent believe it is commonly experienced by women across corporate America.

- Six in ten executive women stated that promotions or transitions to new roles were the times they most experienced imposter syndrome.

- Fully 74 percent of executive women said they don't believe male leaders have as much self-doubt as their female counterparts.

- An overwhelming 81 percent of the executive women surveyed believe they put more pressure on themselves not to fail than men do—in effect, giving themselves a much smaller margin for error than men in similar leadership positions.

We need to constantly remind ourselves that nobody is perfect, and everyone goes into a new position with a little self-doubt and lots of discomfort. It is extremely rare that you can check the box on every requirement and/or skill needed, and that's where the psychological resistance—the self-doubt—comes in. So, you can either run from that resistance or use it to grow, personally and professionally.

I have to "click off" those voices as well. If a new board opportunity comes my way, I might initially think, *But I haven't had all of these career or leadership experiences before.* Then I remind myself of everything I have done, which is more than enough to be a strong contributor. I go in with positivity as opposed to negativity and self-doubt.

$$\bullet \quad \bullet \quad \bullet \quad \bullet \quad \bullet$$

You want to be authentic and you want to be professional, but don't disqualify yourself just because you don't tick all of the boxes!

Don't Focus Solely on the Finances

There is a popular saying in business: "time is money." When you work for a company, you are exchanging your time and your talents for your paycheck. A word of caution: When you're interviewing for a new role, don't make the financial compensation package your sole focus. You need to be passionate about the whole of the role you are considering; otherwise, you'll never be satisfied.

Whether I was interviewing for a new role at Humana or working through a consulting contract with a client, I made sure I followed my own advice.

First and foremost, I need to decide if I'll truly be happy and fulfilled in the role I'm considering. The compensation package requires a delicate balance between what the company is offering and what you believe your value is worth. In my case, when I know a deal is ready to be made, I always ask that my compensation be enough not to distract me but not be so much that it distracts someone else.

My reason is simple: If I go into the negotiations asking for too much, I'm running the risk of having a bull's-eye on my back because I have set a new pay standard. But if I go in asking too little, there will be lingering irritations within me that will distract me from giving 200 percent; my emotional bank account may start out with a negative balance. Find the right balance for *you*, but don't make the dollars the sole focus! (More on this in chapter 4.)

Think Three Moves Ahead

It is human nature to get hung up on progressive and important titles—and bigger paychecks. When we are young, this is called *ambition*, but as we get older, being too absorbed by bigger and bigger and bigger will begin to make you look *selfish* and *self-absorbed*. I recommend focusing on the impact you can make and how that impact will make a difference to the company and to others. Then focus on how this role, these new experiences, leader, and teammates, will ultimately help ladder up to an even bigger impact.

When I counsel young leaders who feel stuck or disenfranchised, I encourage them to think three moves ahead. Where would they like to be in three, five, seven years? I ask them to be very intentional about describing the roles, the team, the impact. Then I ask them to step back into their current reality and focus on how what you do right now, and whom you do it with and for, will pave the way (or ladder up!) to that great position that is three moves out in their career trajectory.

In order to make a meaningful impact that will keep your career successfully sailing for decades, thinking three moves ahead will keep your eyes pointed to the future and help you see the value in the right now. Thinking three moves ahead of where you are right now will help you know what you want to be accountable for and known for as well as the impact you want to make on the business or organization, now and in your all-important future.

Moving ahead doesn't necessarily mean moving to a higher level. Sometimes it necessitates moving sideways, so never discount the value of a lateral move. Much like playing chess, you need to play strategically when planning your career path. And sometimes the best move is a lateral move. A lateral move in business is a career choice that isn't to a level higher but rather to a new role within the same career level. I've taken several lateral moves, and they were some of the best choices I ever made. Each one propelled me forward to that third move out or got me in front of the leader who would get me to that next step (and eventually the third move).

The lesson here is this: don't get hung up on a title or refuse an offer because it's not a direct promotion. You don't always need to progress upward. A lateral move can be a great move, too. Sometimes the lateral moves get you closer to that third move more than a direct promotion would.

Happy Dance Day

If you work your plan, you're going to have success. You're going to have milestone moments along that plan, and there will be those days where you have a happy dance moment.

I recently had lunch with a friend who has a huge leadership position at Humana, someone whom I helped along the way. He talked about a happy dance moment he had recently when his leader called him and said, "I just wanted to tell you, I didn't think I needed somebody in your position. I thought it was superfluous. But you have made my life better, and you've made me more successful." That's a happy dance moment.

A happy dance moment will always make you feel good. And you need those moments to continually remind you of what lights you up and the reason you are in your position.

Conclusion

Your first ninety days will fly by in a blink of an eye. And this time period—whether starting your career, reentering the workforce, or preparing for the third stage of your professional life—will always come with the discomfort of the new. So be prepared, mentally, emotionally, and physically, for the unknowns and the changes you will face. Expect the unexpected. Get comfortable with the uncomfortable. Adjust when necessary. Pivot when needed. Listen and learn. Come in with your ninety-day plan and your business, both of which will give you a road map toward the goals you want to accomplish and how accomplishing those goals will make those around you succeed.

You are in this position for a reason. You are not there by accident. Don't ever forget that! And look forward to all those happy dance moments!

Pattie Dale's Pertinent Points

- If you think about it, being uncomfortable is good for us because it's the starting point in order to learn and grow.

- When you learn to accept the discomfort of the new, you may not enjoy how you feel in the moment, but you can remind yourself that something good, or even big, is about to happen.

- Stepping into a new and challenging role is one of the most important skills you can learn in your career.

- The learning curve looks like this: 1) You don't know what you don't know; 2) you know what you don't know; 3) you learn everything you can about what you don't know; and 4) what you didn't know is now what you know and can do.

- Determining what lights you up—your why—will give you the passion and drive your purpose through the mundane and through the highs and lows that inevitably come with any role you occupy.

- The real reason you are hired for any position is to contribute to the success of others and the overall success of the organization.

- Always remember that you don't need to be the smartest person at the table.

- You never get a second chance to make a first impression.

- You have to *envision* where you want to be. It has to be a reality in your mind before it will become a reality in your life.

- Embrace every happy dance moment that comes your way.

CHAPTER 4

The Money Will Come

I hope you find true meaning, contentment, and passion in your life. I hope you navigate the difficult times and come out with greater strength and resolve. I hope you find whatever balance you seek with your eyes wide open. And I hope that you—yes, you—have the ambition to lean in to your career and run the world. Because the world needs you to change it.
—SHERYL SANDBERG

M oney.

If you think about it, money represents life itself. When we go to work, we give a certain number of hours of our lives to make a set amount of money. We then take that money and spend it on things that are important to us. In this respect, every dollar we earn and spend is a direct representation of what we value in our lives.

When it comes to earning money, "according to recent studies, to be in the top 1% of earners in the U.S., you need to bring in an annual salary of at least $597,815. When it comes to net worth, the top 1% of Americans have a minimum net worth of around $11.1 million."[35]

Kiplinger Online notes the following:[36]

- The top 2 percent have a net worth of $2,472,000.

- The top 5 percent have $1,030,000.

- The top 10 percent have $854,900.

- The top 50 percent have $522,210.

Nerd Wallet reports the following as of 2022:[37]

AGE OF HEAD OF FAMILY	MEDIAN NET WORTH	AVERAGE NET WORTH
Less than 35	$39,000	$183,500
35–44	$135,600	$549,600
45–54	$247,200	$975,800
55–64	$364,500	$1,566,900
65–74	$409,900	$1,794,600
75 plus	$335,600	$1,624,100

These statistics show that most people spend their lives working to earn more money through job promotions, career changes, investments, and other avenues. And more money often affords more ways to demonstrate that we have reached a certain status, live a particular lifestyle, and enjoy specific affluences.

All of the above tells us that the reason we work is to earn a bigger and bigger paycheck.

But I suggest a different reason for working.

The real reason I work isn't to earn more and more money. The real reason I work is to live the life that brings me the most joy and satisfaction. I need to feel accomplished; work gives me that in the deepest sense. I need community; work brings new faces, voices, and energy to my days. I need to give back—be it to a corporate goal, a charitable cause, or a group of teammates who need my help. And I need to live my life in the style I've found most comfortable. Work, and the resulting paycheck, affords me all these things.

Why do *you* work? Think about it, and you can't just say, "It's for the paycheck."

If you think your goal in life is simply to make more money, I can promise you that you'll be distracted from what you're truly aiming for: to create a better and more fulfilling life for yourself.

In my experience, money follows one of two paths: expertise and generosity. The greater our expertise, the more people are willing to pay for it. And to me, the more we are given, the more we are expected to give. Over my career, I have made becoming an expert in a particular role and giving back/generosity the cornerstones and the why of my life.

I'll never forget the Sunday of Memorial Day weekend several years ago. Upon arriving at church, we were all given a button that read, *I know why I work.* That was a great exercise, because most people said, "Well, I work for the money." Then the following question was asked: "*Why* do you need money?" The answers to that were quite literal: mortgage payments, keeping my family comfortable, paying down debt, saving for the future, and so on. But the next layer of whys got to the true point: We work to enable us to have the lives we desire. And life encompasses many things, not just a one-dimensional paycheck.

A Long-Term Perspective

Early in my career, when I was in sales, by my young standards I was making plenty of money. But when I moved into my first staff role at AT&T corporate, my paycheck was cut almost in half. It was then that I had to constantly remind myself that I made this move with a long-term plan to accomplish greater goals and dreams. I knew that if I held pace, that dip would be a momentary monetary blip. And that was true. When I made this move, had I solely focused on my paycheck and the money I would be losing, my life would have gone in a completely different trajectory. If I had made money my goal instead of moving my career forward, instead of having a three-moves-out mindset, I would have made a big mistake.[38]

Over the years, I have known and counseled countless people to look at their long-term goals, and I have said to these same people, "Don't get hung up on the paycheck." When any of us feels scarcity in life, it is a very uncomfortable feeling, and that feeling can easily occur when you focus solely on your paycheck. You may find you get distracted, and even embittered, if you believe you aren't getting paid what you feel you are worth. However, when I've helped people "peel it back" to understand the belief system behind their thoughts, many times it comes down to this notion of *scarcity*; the fear of missing out, that "somebody else gets more than I do," is the driving force.[39]

For your own mental well-being, you must learn to tamp those negative thoughts down and even eradicate that type of thinking from your mind. Those are bad thoughts, especially when you're new to a particular role. You need to avoid anything that could make you bitter, irritable, or distracted from all that you have to do. Trust me: the money will come! Don't get distracted, because money distractions will only cause you grief and hardship. I had to learn this lesson, and I have to continually remind myself of this lesson.

I had to literally put any money distractions in a proverbial box in my mind and tell myself, *This is now on the sideline.* Then I would ask myself, *What else comes with this new opportunity?* Once I was grounded in that thinking, I could open the box and say to myself, *This is what the compensation is now; is that appropriate for the role and for me?* Nine times out of ten, it would be, but had I allowed money to continue to be a distraction, who knows where I would have ended up!

• • • • •

There is so much more treasure in what you get to do over the lifetime of your career than a one-dimensional paycheck. You're going to make friends for life. You're going to use your mind in ways you never thought you would, with the dividend of having a healthy brain throughout your lifetime.

No matter what phase you are in, look out your career "window," because where you are today and whatever you are doing is going to serve you for many decades. During each step of your career, you are stretching your capacity to learn and grow; you're meeting new people and going to new places, all of which contribute to having a fulfilling career—and life! You get to experience all of this, *and* get a paycheck. And guess what? Your paycheck will grow along with you!

The Beauty of a Lateral Move

In chapter 3, I noted that sometimes the best move is a lateral move. A lateral move in business is a career step that isn't to a level higher but into a new role at the same level.

Throughout your career, you will be presented with lateral moves, and you might question whether such a move is in your best interest; you are not necessarily being promoted but taking a position that is equal to your current position.

It is easy to bristle at the thought of making a lateral move because it goes against our natural tendency to want to move upward. But, just like chess strategy, sometimes your best move is a lateral one that will set you up to be stronger for the long game—and the long game is where you see yourself in the next several months and years and at the end of your career.

Over my professional life, I've made several lateral moves that gave me a great depth of experience. These moves always helped me ladder up because of the education, the new skills, the new leaders, and the experience I would be able to bring with me to my next role. This meant I needed to put as much effort into my lateral move as I would had I received a promotion. Laterals are what I call "precious cargo," so do not overlook the potential advantage they offer. Don't get distracted by any lack of compensation or other benefits.

A lateral move can make you a stronger candidate for other career moves, so don't hesitate at making such a move if you can see the possibility of it benefitting you in the long run.

• • • • •

When I was promoted to a big role at Humana's headquarters, the insurance industry was going through huge changes from a regulatory perspective. It was a tricky time for our industry, and for Humana. Only a year into this big new role, Humana made the correct decision to consolidate its large and small business segments, and the consolidation left me without a role.

Now *that* felt like scarcity! But there were leaders in my network who were looking out for me. I quickly received an offer to take the position of market president, the position I held before coming to corporate headquarters. Instead, I chose to take a lateral move into something completely different—I chose to move from Humana's commercial space into the Medicare space within the company at a time when Humana was investing heavily in Medicare. This lateral move allowed me to learn so much and gain experience I never would have acquired, which in turn increased my value to my company and myself. I reported directly to Humana's chief operating officer with a great mission before me and highly visible work, and I was surrounded by an excellent team.

Part of my brand (more on that later) is being very connected to the communities where I live and work. Being known by that brand was key to my being offered this new, great role; it required much greater work at the community level. It was work that allowed the blending of physician care with community care. And it was a perfect combination of all my skills, interests, and what I had learned about the work of Humana over the last decade. This role truly defined *why* I worked. It was the best decision and lateral move I could have made, but had I let my ego get in the way and been distracted by the "lateral," I would have missed the chance of a lifetime!

LATERAL MOVES AND COMPENSATION

When you make a lateral career move, you are "in the game" because of the skills and experience you bring to the table. But a word of caution: this lateral role may not have a bump in compensation. Don't get distracted by that, but perhaps suggest that your new leader reexamine your compensation after you've had enough time to prove your worth. Instead, look at the role as a whole, not just as a chance to receive a potential change in compensation.

Becoming an Expert

No matter where your career takes you, becoming an expert in your field will make you stand out in the crowd and increase your earning potential. Being an expert in a particular field with specialized knowledge, skills, and experience will make you the preferred job candidate or increase your value within your current organization.

What makes someone an expert? There is no definitive answer, because roles and responsibilities have different definitions within industries. However, in his classic book *Outliers: The Story of Success*, Malcolm Gladwell repeatedly refers to the "ten-thousand-hour rule," noting that the key to achieving true expertise is a matter of *correctly* practicing a particular skill, or having been in a particular role, for at least ten thousand hours.[40]

Practically speaking, that means about 4.5 years in the work world to become an expert at simply working. Overlay a specific set of skills and expertise on top, and you are closer to eight to ten years before you are an expert. You'll need to put in the time, so make sure you have the underlying passion for pursuing this particular set of skills, make sure that everything ladders up, and be prepared for the times of discomfort. But with expertise, your value will be very apparent, and the money surely will come!

In an insightful article written for *Forbes* magazine, senior contributor Bernhard Schroeder notes that data in a study conducted by the US Bureau of Labor Statistics shows that people between eighteen and forty-eight on average held 11.7 jobs.[41] Given that it takes four to five years to become an expert at something, this statistic makes me think that the number of experts within an industry is definitely decreasing, while the number of generalists is increasing! For experts, there is a growing opportunity to stand out!

Schroeder also lists the following skills that experts cultivate:[42]

- Redefine Your Network

  Jim Rohn, personal development guru, says, "You are the average of the five people you spend the most time with."

- Become a Thought Leader

  Never be content with the status quo; always be looking for the next evolution of your profession by pushing boundaries, trying new techniques, and adding value.

- Share Your Knowledge

  Experts are willing to serve their professional community to benefit all.

- Rigorously Follow Trends

  Experts stay at the forefront of new trends in their industry, providing themselves with foresight so they can take advantage of change. You can set up specific Google alerts, subscribe to specific trend blogs, and check in on websites like TrendHunter.

- Never Stop Learning

  Experts never "arrive" and are committed lifetime learners—through reading books, attending workshops and seminars, obtaining additional educational degrees, and more.

I'm a big fan of the *Harvard Business Review* (*HBR*) to give me insights into how I can enhance my career. I recently read an interesting article in *HBR* that I feel makes some poignant points on how to become an expert. Freelance contributor Michelle Gibbons writes about benefits of creating a "Career Guide: a well-thought-out plan highlighting what it will take to progress our careers in ways that we find truly meaningful." Gibbons states this is a four-part plan and that "the ultimate goal is to identify and take steps that will help you align your career with your deeper purpose and skills" and will set you up to become an expert in your field.[43]

The four parts to Gibbons's plan are as follows:[44]

- Part 1: Write down your current "career traps."
  These are patterns of thinking and behavior that are automatic because they are familiar to us, but they can have a negative "impact on our productivity and effectiveness and lead to poor health as well as feelings of isolation."

- Part 2: Define your purpose.
  Gibbons reiterates what Seth Goden says about knowing your why: your purpose is your why—the reason you do what you do. She notes that the starting point is to "pay attention to what matters to you and motivates you" and to ask yourself, *Why do I do what I do?*

- Part 3: Document your unique skills, and create your selling statement.
  This step involves taking the time to think about, identify, and write out your "unique skills or your Unique Selling Point (USP)—the things that, combined, make you better than your competition and would make any hiring manager pick you."

- Part 4: Seize opportunities to expand yourself.
  Every opportunity that comes your way is a potential open door to ladder up. The key word is *potential*, meaning that you are not meant to say yes to every opportunity that comes

along; let your intuition and experience guide you in being strategic.

SOFT SKILLS

As you continue to develop your expertise, don't forget about the value of the soft skills you have. Soft skills are multidisciplinary and will benefit you personally and professionally. Over the years, I have found that developing key soft skills such as emotional intelligence—identifying, understanding, and recognizing biases, assumptions, and judgments—has helped me throughout my career.[45]

The Beauty of Generosity

I'm fond of the Charles Dickens classic *A Christmas Carol*. The main character, Ebenezer Scrooge, is a wealthy businessman and a miserable miser. Scrooge's assistant, Bob Cratchit, is just the opposite: poor, yet happy. However, one Christmas Eve, when three ghosts appear to show Scrooge his past, present, and future life, he has a complete change of heart. From that Christmas morning on, he dedicates his life to "live to give." In other words, Scrooge learns the beauty of generosity.

Generosity is something I learned from my parents. I can remember my mother constantly giving of her precious time and resources. If she saw a child in my class who needed a coat and/or shoes, she went out of her way to meet the need. She also volunteered to drive people to medical appointments several towns away when those very sick individuals had no other way to get to their appointments.

The same thing is true of my father. He was very community oriented. Growing up during the Great Depression and fighting in World War II made an indelible impression on him. He always understood how much he had, that he really didn't have scarcity, that his family always had enough. But he talked about seeing children sleeping on the streets; he witnessed the scarcity that gripped our nation during the Great Depression. I believe it's what drove him to be generous and to always remember the needs of others. He knew what a gift it was to be able to share with others.

One poignant memory I have from my childhood through my young adult years is an event that occurred every Christmas Eve. My father gathered our family, and together we made little brown bag stockings and filled them with fruit and magazines and combs and candy to give to prisoners at the local jail. My dad didn't want anyone, regardless of circumstances, waking up without the blessing of Christ and Christmas on that special morning. There was also a "tagline" for each of us, given daily. He would remind us to "remember the needs of others." This powerful phrase has stayed with me throughout my adult life and professional career. It is part of every prayer I offer.

• • • • •

In a corporate environment, the beauty of generosity means that you are not in it for yourself only. Giving back—through helping a coworker, leading or participating in a volunteer effort, mentoring, or simply taking the time to listen to those who lead you or whom you lead—brings with it its own reward. Your career sits within a connectional environment. You are not on your career path simply to enhance your own life. Giving back your time, your talent, your skills, your treasure, your knowledge and experience will make your life more meaningful, because you are connecting with others to fill voids in their space, and that, in turn, will help you fill your own voids.

I've made giving back an integral part of all that I do, and it has never failed to make a huge difference in both my personal and professional life!

Pattie Dale's Pertinent Points

- The real reason you work isn't to earn more and more money. The real reason you work is to live the life that brings you the most joy and satisfaction.

- It's important to "peel it back" to understand the belief system behind your thoughts about money and compensation. Many times, it comes down to this notion of *scarcity*: the fear of missing out and that "somebody else gets more than I do."

- Sometimes your best move is a lateral one that will set you up to be stronger for the long game—and the long game is where you see yourself in the next several months and years and at the end of your career.

- Make becoming an expert in a particular role and giving back/generosity whenever and however you can the cornerstones of your career.

CHAPTER 5

Suddenly Sunday

Sundays should come with a pause button.
—ANONYMOUS

L ike most people, I love my weekends! I love the freedom, love to be awakened by my circadian rhythm, love to do just what I want to do, on my schedule, and with my favorite person, Jim Tye!

But on Sunday morning, an email might come in or something else work related. It's then I realize that the world is going to come roaring back and in a few short hours it will be Monday morning. My freedom will be gone, and it's back to the structured, scheduled, demanding life of work. While I truly love my work life, Sunday can often seem to arrive far too quickly and make Monday's work seem much, much bigger. I know I'm not alone in this thinking and feeling. Often called the "Sunday Scaries," the website Headspace notes the following:[46]

> The Sunday Scaries (or Sunday blues, as they're sometimes called) are feelings of anxiety or dread that happen the day before heading back to work. According to a LinkedIn

survey, 80 percent of professionals say they experience the Sunday Scaries, with over 90 percent of Millennials and Gen Z reporting they feel it.

What is the cure?[47]

Over the years I have found a few hacks and facts to help my weekend joy last a little bit longer and to help me see Mondays in a more positive light:

- Be intentional about discerning what is causing you this dread of Monday. Name it. If it's a particular meeting you dread having on Monday (I've had millions of those!), make sure you are well prepared before you end your workday on Friday. Then, when that feeling of dread pops up on Sunday, you can quickly remind yourself that you are fully prepared. Preparation for Mondays before you leave the work world on Fridays will preserve *many* Sundays.

- Did you know that the majority of heart attacks occur on Monday?[48] This tells all of us the importance of unplugging on Sunday.[49] Perhaps it also highlights the fact that so many people dread Monday.

- The word *Monday* literally means "day of the moon." Some explain this to mean it is the first day in which we can step into our potential and to use our intuition to safeguard us through the rest of the week. The fact is, we *need* Mondays!

- Schedule something good to happen on Monday. Go to a movie Monday evening, go out to dinner, take a dance class … do something you can look forward to.

- Go gently into Monday by getting a great Sunday night's rest. Focus on your self-care on Sunday. Go to church if that gives you peace and joy, cook a great meal, take a walk—take care of yourself!

- If it is comfortable for you, meditate. Meditation "can help us manage our thoughts so we can snap ourselves back into being more present and stress less about the week ahead."[50]

- Think about Monday and going back to work as something you *get* to do rather than something you *have* to do. It is amazing what recognizing our freedom of choice has to do with our attitude.

- Count your blessings on Sunday night, and take the time to pray. Wrap the weekend on a positive note, and think about the people in your life whom you love, and who love you. Think about the fact that whatever work you do during the week helps you to support and care for those special people. Work really is a blessing in life—if you know *why* you work (and you can't say, "For the paycheck!").

When you get back to work on Monday, remember that your team is probably feeling the stress of Monday too. Be kind to your team, your leader, and those you lead, and try to keep their Sundays soft. Do you really have to send that email on Sunday, or can you wait until the work world begins again tomorrow?

Ask yourself, *What can I do to change the perception of Mondays? What can I do to make Mondays a great day to come in to work?* When you're the one in charge—and you will be—remember, before they leave on Friday, thank them for their contributions, tell them to have a great weekend, and tell them how much you look forward to seeing them again on Monday.

Don't Let the Grumpy Ones into Your Thoughts on Sunday

Just as I've experienced, you'll have different kinds of people in your work life. Whether they're a leader, manager, or coworker, some are kind, considerate, and generous. Others are simply not. They aren't happy with life and certainly not with work life. Don't let their mood or attitude ruin your day—especially your Sunday.

Think about this: When other people negatively affect your day, you are giving them the power to control you. Is that what you really want—to have someone else in control? Living life by your own principles, values, and beliefs gives you power and control over your attitudes, actions, and responses, all of which tell you that *you* are in control of you—not someone else. Yes, you are going to see those grumpy ones on Monday. Yes, they are still going to be grumpy. But why does their grumpiness determine the quality of your Sunday? In fact, why are you even giving them any thought at all?

Instead of replaying negative conversations over and over again, try the following to help you maintain your peace and positivity on Sunday:

- Remember, their grumpiness is about them, not you. Don't take their negativity as a personal affront; more than likely their mood has nothing to do with you.

- Set boundaries by being mindful about your interactions and conversations during the coming week. Keep your connection to Mr. or Ms. Grumpy to a minimum whenever you realize they are in a bad mood. Limit your one-on-one time, and have someone else with you whenever possible.

- Don't be the source of gossip about this person!

- Think of ways you can express positivity toward the individual. Are there ways you can express gratitude? Can you show kindness or generosity?

- Remind yourself that you don't walk in their shoes and you have no idea what pressure they might be under or what is going on in their personal life.

- Change the atmosphere. Negative, grumpy people know they are like this. Think of ways you can help them feel less judged, criticized, or even dismissed. You can be the glass-half-full person!

Never Check Email in the Morning— Especially on Sunday Morning

One of my favorite books is *Never Check E-Mail in the Morning*, by Julie Morgenstern. One of the principles she writes is to be intentional about how you want your day to go and what you want to accomplish … before ever starting your day.[51]

Before I finish my workday—or work week—I always look forward to what needs to be accomplished the next day or the next week. I organize my thoughts around it, make lists, put in calendar entries—anything I can do to hit the ground running without trauma the following day or the following week.

When you have your day or week planned before checking emails, you are approaching the day in a proactive versus a reactive manner. Don't you agree that one feels much better than the other? When you are proactive, you can adjust, but when you are reactive, you are at the mercy of whatever comes along. Being reactive feels like you are the silver ball in a pinball machine, being battered from one task to another. However, being intentionally proactive with your attitude and with what you're going to accomplish will not only feel better but help you produce better results. And doing this on Friday will make your Sunday much more peace filled.

Don't Put Off until Sunday What You Can Do Today!

Take a lesson from me, and learn to *compartmentalize*. Work will always have a never-ending list of demands. I used to agonize over a never-ending list of things to do. Fortunately, I read a great little book years ago titled *Don't Sweat the Small Stuff*,[52] which helped me realize that you actually never want your inbox empty. You always want to have the next thing to work on, the next place to travel, the next restaurant to visit, and so on.

But dealing with the never-empty work inbox takes some strategic thinking. For me, this means sitting down and recognizing what I want/need/have to get done, then prioritizing those items.[53] If I have work to do on a Saturday, it's better for my psyche to sit down and get it done first thing in the morning so that the rest of the day and the rest of the weekend are free; I don't want the work drifting over to Sunday. And while you're thinking about how to compartmentalize, try not to expect those you lead/manage to do work over their weekend unless there is an urgency or emergency. You're in charge, so be kind and respectful, and remember that your folks need an unplugged break as much as you do.

One of my leaders, Beth Bierbower, put into play something she referred to as *digital detox*, meaning from 5:00 p.m. Friday until 8:00 a.m. Sunday, she and her team could not send emails. That seems simple, but doing so accomplished two things. First, it made us much more efficient in the Monday-to-Friday game, and we didn't build up lots of work to tackle on Saturday and Sunday.

Second, it meant I could untether from work email for the weekend. Before digital detox, I never knew what request would come in when, so I was constantly checking email and text. After digital detox, I knew I could check email when it was comfortable for me. Since it was highly likely there would be no work emails—unless something urgent that required my attention had occurred—digital detox became a beautiful thing!

Always remember that in this always-on world, you and your team need the chance to unplug!

• • • • •

Sunday is a very special day of the week, and I treat it as a precious treasure. But I had to learn to prepare for Sunday on Friday so that I could keep the grumpy people out of my mind all weekend. I had to learn to compartmentalize, to maintain a digital detox and let others and myself unplug. And when the inevitable Scary Sunday thoughts try to infiltrate my mind, I remind myself of why I love going to work on Monday!

Pattie Dale's Pertinent Points

- When you get back to work on Monday, remember that your team is probably feeling the stress of Monday too. Be kind to your team, your leader, and those you lead, and try to keep their Sundays soft.

- When other people negatively affect your day, you are giving them the power to control you. Is that what you really want—to have someone else in control?

- When you have your day or week planned before checking emails, you are approaching the day in a proactive versus reactive manner.

- You're in charge, so be kind and respectful, and remember that your folks need an unplugged break as much as you do.

CHAPTER 6

Up by the Bootstraps

I get knocked down, but I get up again!
—CHUMBAWAMBA

I'm not an offensive person. I tend to get along with almost everyone and do my best to be very kind and empathetic. I make a solid effort to walk in someone's shoes in order to understand their journey, their position.

I love being a leader and all the responsibilities that come with leadership. I've never been a dictator. I've never been a screamer. I am a firm believer that teamwork always outperforms individual work. Yes, everyone has to do their own great work, but individual work must ladder up to the overall success of the team. As a leader, this is what I've always tried to model. That model had always treated me well, until ...

At the start of my career as market president with Humana, I was so excited about this new opportunity to learn and lead in a new industry, to work with new and smart leaders, and to succeed at the challenge to turn the market around. When I walked into the office the first morning, there were seventy-five people in the room, and they actually applauded. While not expecting such a positive reception, I knew this team had been without a market president for months, and this reaction confirmed that they were ready for leadership! I took time to introduce myself; tell them about my life, my family, my career journey; and then affirm that I wanted this group to succeed and succeed as a team. I did know enough about the challenges to build a business plan, and I was ready to also build out my ninety-day plan.

Later that day, I began meetings with my direct reports and the market leadership team. The first three meetings went very well. The leaders came prepared with their goals and objectives, their current concerns, and suggestions regarding clients, brokers, or partners with whom I should meet. But the last two meetings were quite different. It was clear these two leaders were offended that I had even been given the market president role. How could I, who had zero experience in "their industry," be their leader? It was clear they were not supporters, but I had no idea they would be such detractors! And within the market, they were both very influential leaders.

During those initial meetings and in the days to come, I reminded myself that if I held on and remembered what my leader told me—"This is a marathon, not a sprint"—that I would either win over these key leaders or move on without them. And as it happened, one self-selected out, and one stayed in the business. And my personal blessing is that they both stay in touch with me, and I know I've made a big difference in their lives. But I didn't have the luxury of knowing this when I first started. It was such a hard walk from the parking garage and then down the hallway every morning to my office, knowing that I had two very powerful people who were extreme detractors.

I'm a believer in *not* going it alone; I comfortably and routinely seek advice from others I trust and respect. After getting settled into my new position, I decided to form an informal board of directors of other women business leaders who had succeeded in this market. In those days there weren't many of us, and I realized that we could help and support one another. I also hired an outside coach, Karen McCullough, with whom I created a ninety-day plan, and then we worked the plan.[54]

As a leadership team, together we read the book *5 Dysfunctions of a Team*, by Patrick Lencioni, and worked with Karen on how we each contributed to the dysfunction and what we could do to move from dysfunctional to high performing. In my case, it took some time to move the trust needle with the two difficult leaders, but by mile sixteen, we had an easy and effective working relationship.

During my time with my informal board of directors, several important leadership traits came to the surface. Over the years, these traits have served me well in both my personal and professional life:

✔ RESILIENCE

I realize now that in those days I had what is called *resilience*. To me, resilience is being able to stand back up and keep moving forward after you've been knocked down by the unexpected. Resilience was certainly my ally during my early days at Humana. I also recall there were lots of prayers along that journey. I had no doubt that God had put me right where he wanted me. It was up to me to gather and marshal the resources I needed to do the work that needed to be done. I reminded myself that people had invested in me, taken a chance on me, and I was determined not to let them down.

I love this quote by Taiki Matsuura: "Despite all the talk about resilience being an individual trait, most of us are only as resilient as we are loved."[55]

✔ CONFIDENCE

Speaking of being loved, my siblings and I were fortunate to have parents who instilled confidence in us as children and young adults. I think confidence is an underrated yet beautiful gift that any parent can give a child. It's also a terrible, even cruel disservice to take away someone's confidence, because doing so can hold someone back their entire life and throughout their chosen work path. I can tell you with certainty that I never would have been resilient if I didn't have *confidence*. As a leader, I look for every opportunity to instill confidence in people, whether they are part of my team or someone else's, or even if they work in another organization.

✔ SELF-DISCIPLINE

I would say that *self-discipline* is the foundation on which resilience and confidence are built. Merriam-Webster defines self-discipline as the "correction or regulation of oneself for the sake of improvement."[56] Here's a great quote that exemplifies self-discipline: "Mastering others is strength; mastering yourself is true power."[57]

For me, self-discipline comes easiest when I have a goal or incentive attached to it. For example, preparing to run a marathon meant I had to avoid late nights to get in my early-morning training runs. I had to give up eating junk but fun food on Friday in order to make sure my body was ready for my Saturday long runs every single week leading up to the marathon. It took self-discipline to say no to foods that would affect my physical ability because, as everyone knows, fun foods are ... fun!

In the work world, self-discipline includes being careful and intentional about your work and remembering that how you go about it impacts others. This takes commitment and repetition, two foundational factors for self-discipline. Commitment means keeping your word; it means sticking with it. It means not giving up, even if it gets tough, and doing what you've said you would do. Repetition means being consistent in the way you show up and in what you do so that others know they can depend on you. Keep in mind that self-discipline is more mental than physical; most hindrances to self-discipline are mental blocks and rarely physical limitations.

Here are some ways I've learned to overcome my mental blocks:

- Challenge Perceptions

  There is a saying: "Perception is our reality, but our reality isn't always our perception." Perceived limitations need to be challenged to see if they are real—if so, what can be done to overcome them?—or simply an excuse not to do something. Whenever your self-discipline is challenged, always ask yourself, *What's going on in my mind? What am I thinking? How am I interpreting the situation I'm in? How can I remove whatever is causing me to stand still versus move forward?*

- Find What Motivates You

  Name it, and write it down. At times, it can be hard to concentrate on a task or project, and there are times when procrastination sets in. But if you keep your motivation in the forefront of your mind, you will find the inner strength to follow through.

- Take a Break

  Sometimes you simply need to step away from what you are doing to give yourself a mental break. Going for a walk to clear your mind or doing something that is not related to whatever you are focused on can give you renewed energy.

- Forgive

  There are times we all mentally and verbally beat ourselves up; that's part of being human. However, self-discipline requires that you forgive yourself—and that you forgive others—of any shortcomings. As Alexander Pope said, "To err is human; to forgive is divine."[58] Another great quote around this topic is from Jim Tye: "When you lose, and there are times you will, never lose the lesson." When we learn from our mistakes, we build up the self-discipline not to repeat them.

✔ CURIOSITY

On November 26, 2011, as part of its Mars Science Laboratory mission, NASA launched *Curiosity*, the largest and most capable rover ever sent to Mars. "*Curiosity* set out to answer the question: Did Mars ever have the right environmental conditions to support small life forms called microbes?"[59]

Just like this rover, being curious is all about keeping an open mind to "What if?" and "Why is that?" questions that spark new ideas and new ways of thinking, which lead to new ways of doing.

As evidenced by our history of exploration, inventions, and continuous improvements, humankind is naturally curious. While some people are more curious than others, we all have what is called a "curiosity meter." Curiosity leads us to learn and understand; it is the reason we explore profound mysteries such as space, why we want to know even more about our planet, Earth; it is a driving force for meeting other people. Curiosity gets the credit for the reason we are always moving forward in life. Curiosity sparks hope for a better life for ourselves and for future generations.

If you think about it, from toddler to adult, learning and growing happen because we are curious. It makes us think, imagine, and question so we can broaden our horizons. Curiosity isn't driven by right or wrong questions but by the desire to explore, to question, to experience, and to understand. Larry Senn, author of *The Mood Elevator*, has created the Mood Elevator meter card, which I've grown fond of. Knowing my mood helps me determine my level of curiosity on any given day.

The Mood Elevator

How we feel when
we are our best self

— Grateful
— Wise, insightful
— Creative, innovative
— Resourceful
— Hopeful, optimistic
— Appreciative, compassionate
— Patient, understanding
— Sense of humor
— Flexible, adaptive, cooperative
— Curious, interested
— Impatient, frustrated
— Irritated, bothered
— Worried, anxious
— Defensive, insecure
— Judgmental, blaming
— Self-righteous
— Stressed, burned-out
— Angry, hostile
— Low, depressed

How we feel when
we are off our game

Larry Senn, The Mood Elevator, accessed December 12, 2023, https://themoodelevator.com/. Used with permission.

I'm also fond of Dr. Debra Clary's work on curiosity. Dr. Clary has developed the Curiosity Curve®, and on her website she notes several points of impact that curiosity has on an organization:[60, 61]

- *Innovation:* Curiosity can lead to the exploration of new ideas, technologies, and methods, fostering innovation within the organization.

- *Problem solving:* Curious individuals are more likely to seek out solutions and alternative approaches to challenges, driving effective problem solving.

- *Learning and development:* A culture of curiosity encourages continuous learning and development as individuals and teams seek to expand their knowledge and skills.

- *Engagement:* Curious employees are often more engaged with their work, as they are naturally motivated to explore and understand their tasks and projects.

- *Adaptability:* Curiosity enables individuals and teams to adapt to changing circumstances and market conditions, helping the organization stay relevant and competitive.

- *Collaboration*: Curiosity can facilitate collaboration and knowledge sharing among employees as they seek to learn from each other's experiences and expertise.

If I can train myself to stay curious, I find myself more energized, happy, and purpose driven. Consistently, I find that when I am irritable, tired, or "done with" a topic or project, it is because I've lost my curiosity about it. I have to step away and then step back into the task, project, or conversation with a mindset of curiosity.

Curiosity is a beautiful reminder that we'll never know everything. It's a reminder that you should never assume that you know everything about the work you've been doing for the last year, the spouse you've been married to for thirty-three years, or your sister or brother who has been in your life for sixty-five years. Staying curious keeps you in a positive mindset and energized about future potential.

✔ CREDIBILITY

Credibility goes hand in hand with authenticity. Credibility is the proof that you can do what you've been asked to do. Authenticity means you are true to your own personality, values, and spirit, regardless of the pressure to act otherwise; credibility is the proof you are being your authentic self. When I was hired at Humana, even though I had no experience or credibility in healthcare, I had credibility as a successful leader in other industries and had brought them to profitability, which is why I was brought into the company. I could be credible in my leadership because I had proof in the rearview mirror.

✔ BE REALLY GOOD AT SEVERAL "SPORTS"

In the early days of my career, a wise leader gave me this advice: be an athlete. If you think about the really athletic people you know, chances are strong that they are capable of competing well in several sports. What this leader meant with her counsel to me was that I needed to become good and become known in several different business disciplines: sales, product management, strategy, and so on. That "athleticism" would allow me to pivot to another role much more easily and would also allow me to quickly understand more holistically what my peers and leaders were working to accomplish.

There is some wonderful research around the subject of corporate athletes. Writing for Jumpstart, Alinda Gupta notes the following:[62]

> Corporate athletes are business leaders who have to constantly cope with unprecedented demands in the workplace and have the physical strength to do so. Loehr and Schwartz coined the term "corporate athletes" in 2001, shining a

light on integrating the mind, body, spirit and emotions for optimum workplace performance.

Gupta adds, "The corporate athlete model ensures that you are optimizing all aspects of your lifestyle" and enables you to 1) perform at your full potential; 2) have long-term success; and 3) effectively recover from stressful situations.[63]

At AT&T, the best C-suite leaders had five "athletic" experiences: start up a business, rebuild a business, take down a business, launch a new product, and build a distribution channel. Talk about business athleticism!

Being an athlete in the corporate world means that you are not typecast. You are known as someone who can do many things, not just one! The further up the corporate ladder you aspire to climb, the more well rounded your business experiences need to be. Not every athletic experience will be a pleasant one. But each one will make you a stronger leader.

While at ChaseCom, I had the good fortune to work with a brilliant person, Mary Logan, who to this day is still a dear friend. Mary was ChaseCom's CFO, and I was the COO. We made a really great team, and I have tons of memories of our working together to build a great business for our owners/founders. One particular task, however, was not much fun. Under pressure for more revenues and lower expenses, Mary and I were tasked with understanding which of our markets was not thriving and then determining whether we should continue with the market or shut it down.

After much careful analysis, we had to make the painful decision to close a particular market, giving notice to our employees that their roles were going away. I was the one who owned communicating, and for me—or anyone who has had to do this—it is the worst part of a job. While it was through no fault of their own, I had to look people in the eyes and say, "We have to close this market." I can remember saying that to one particular employee, who looked at me in panic and said, "I just made an offer on a house. I won't even be able to get a mortgage if I don't have a job." I can still see his face today.

There are going to be times when you have to have that type of very difficult experience. I can tell you that it makes you stronger on the other side. How? Because you learn how to build your business so that you never have to have that conversation again. You learn how to do a better job testing, market testing, and finding out if this product will be successful in this market so that you don't have to pull out of a market again. Difficult experiences teach you to be better at building the next business because of the one you had to tear down.

Up by the Bootstraps

I can't even begin to tell you how many mistakes I've made over my career. But I can tell you that if I had let these same mistakes dwell in my mind for too long, I would have limited my career in one way or another. *Up by the bootstraps* means that I have to plant my two feet on the ground every day, remember what I'm called to do, and go do it, even on days when it doesn't feel good to keep moving forward.

I know there will be days when I'm going to get on calls that will be very uncomfortable. There will be many of those days in your career. But if you learn to marshal your resilience and your resources and to be well prepared, then you, too, will put your feet on the ground and walk forward because people are depending on you. In this way, pulling myself up by the bootstraps has become embedded in my muscle memory.

When I was a child, we had a toy called a Weeble. They were egg shaped, and when they were tipped over, a weight in the bottom center caused the toy to rise up again. There was a catchphrase used in advertising Weebles that applies today: "Weebles wobble but they don't fall down."[64]

This is a great illustration of pulling yourself up by the bootstraps. That's how you have to go about your work life; you're going to get knocked down, and you have to stand back up and keep walking. People are depending on you, and you have work to do; you have a role to occupy and others to help move forward, others to lead. So, you can't simply fall down when the going gets tough. You've got to pull yourself up by the bootstraps.

Pattie Dale's Pertinent Points

- Think about forming your own informal board of directors of other business leaders who have succeeded in your market, your industry, your role, etc.

- Consider how you can develop the six checks of resilience, confidence, self-discipline, curiosity, credibility, and being a business athlete in your career.

- *Up by the bootstraps* means that you have to plant your two feet on the ground every day, remember what you are called to do, and go do it, even on days when you don't feel good or it doesn't feel good to keep moving forward.

CHAPTER 7

Polish That Brand

*Your brand is what people say about you
when you're not in the room.*
—JEFF BEZOS

N o matter where you are in your career, your personal brand is of utmost importance. Your personal brand is what you stand for, what you are known for. It is the ongoing culmination of the experiences, skills, and values that differentiate you from those around you. For example, I've learned over the years that my personal branding attributes are *high positive energy, executive presence, and authentic approachability.* The combination of these three attributes is why I believe so many people reach out to me for career guidance. Helping others in their journey absolutely lights me up, which is the main reason I'm writing this book.

During my six years at Humana's headquarters, I had a steady stream of young men and women leaders who needed guidance and support with career decisions, were having difficulty with their own leaders and team members, or were dealing with the omnipresent "I have this offer, but should I take it?" dilemma. I never turned down an opportunity to meet with these folks, and one of the first areas we worked to uncover was "'What are you known for?" or "What is your brand?" It is paramount that you identify and constantly *polish* your brand. A polished personal brand makes it clear to others who you are and who you are not. At Humana, I would get calls or emails from other senior leaders saying, "Can I send so-and-so to talk to you? Will you give her some mentoring and some coaching? She needs some Pattie Dale."

When this first started happening, I wasn't sure what they meant by "some Pattie Dale." Regardless, I would always show up to our meetings as professional and approachable with a positive, high-energy attitude about helping those I met with. It took me some time to realize this was my personal brand, how others saw me. I was being authentic in my desire to add value to the individuals I met with and mentored. This way of giving back and being generous was/is a highlight of my day!

Identify and Develop Your Brand

Identifying and developing your brand starts with having a solid understanding of what lights you up. This will tell you what you're passionate about and what you're gifted and skilled at. As stated earlier, my brand is having executive presence, being very approachable, and having very high positive energy. Being approachable and having high energy have been part of my DNA all my life, and those attributes have served me well when it came to building my brand. Most leaders or teammates don't want to fear approaching you for an answer or an assignment, and to run at the pace required in most roles these days, high energy is a true plus! But executive presence was a brand I had to work on over the years.

It started with that age-old adage to watch and model those you admire who are moving up the ranks. I did just that, and I did it well before I had anything close to an executive title. I showed up prepared, and I dressed in a way that suited my style but also modeled those I felt I should emulate. I worked on being confident in new settings and making and following up on introductions. All of those were learned, not natural. But they all came together and allowed me to claim those as brand attributes. Sometimes there are brand attributes you wish for, but they simply don't stick or surface as strongly as others. One of those for me is analytics. I *love* analytics. Through logical reasoning, critical thinking, communication, research, data analysis, and creativity, I've been able to take complicated information, reconstruct it into smaller categories, and then draw conclusions.

In other words, I have the ability to take the complex and make it simple. Throughout my career, I've continued to develop my analytical skills when dealing with facts and figures and when working with people. But I will tell you that the analytical skills I have and love never fully surfaced as part of my brand attributes when I was at my highest career spot. There were so many others whose skill in that space was much stronger. However, that doesn't make analytical skills any less important or impactful to me, because the use of that skill lights me up! Whatever they are, your passion, gifts, and skills should put you in a more visible place when those passions, gifts, and skills begin to define who you are. To develop those identifiable skills and talents, don't just limit yourself to your workplace. Look outside to see where you can develop your personal brand.

In chapter 6, I mentioned the notion of being an athlete. This is important because it hearkens back to the first way your personal brand will be identifiable. In your career, your "athletic" skills are transferable skills. For example, you've been a great success selling your organization's product. Now you're ready to move into product development.

Initially, someone might say, "You've been quite the success in sales, but product management is quite different." However, you are a corporate athlete; you've developed talents and skills that are transferable into other areas. You—or better yet, your supporters—will say, "Yes, but do you know how well I can articulate our mission? Do you know how well he can cost justify a solution? Do you know how much taller she stands out in that field of sales? All these skills make him/her capable of transitioning to product management or product leadership."

At Humana, I was asked to meet with the CEO regarding an opportunity that ultimately led me to Louisville, Humana's corporate headquarters. The question posed to me was this: "I can see that you are capable of running a few large markets, but can you run an entire national footprint? Can you handle the work of making this segment profitable?"

I had prepared for these challenges to the value and skill I had, so I was able to speak confidently and with solid examples that illustrated my transferable skills. And I got the double promotion! My personal brand and my transferable skills have been the wind at my back throughout my career journey. Find the way to develop *your* personal brand, either inside your organization or through a favorite "learning lab" within community organizations. There are plenty of organizations that will welcome your help, and I promise that if you take a leadership role within those organizations, you'll have plenty of polish for your brand.

A wise woman, Ellie Francisco, told me a long time ago, "Don't just sit on a board. Don't just sit on a committee. Take a leadership role, because that's where you will get strong at being accountable, and that's where you will get known." Using outside-the-company or outside-the-organization avenues to develop and polish your brand is a fabulous thing and a rich resource lab.

How can you take your gifts, talents, skills, and experience and learn how to lead with them and be known for them within a community organization? This is a beautiful learning lab, and throughout my career, my involvement in different nonprofit organizations has helped me attain new leadership skills, promotions, and professional opportunities. Ultimately that work, combined with the work I was fortunate to do during my career, got me noticed and helped me attain one of the best roles I've ever had in my life—leading Humana's Bold Goal work.[66]

Doing so was a twofer, allowing me to be giving back while giving me the opportunity to build and polish my brand and reputation in a very authentic way.

Early in my career, I heard the expression, "People should hear your footsteps in the hall." Another way of saying this is "The best leaders are still there even when they have left the room."

What this means is that you are so draped over the work, over your team, over the division you lead that others feel your steadying hand and guidance even when you aren't around. You don't develop this by micromanaging; you develop this because you've fortified your team, your product, your assigned tasks, and you can walk away knowing that your world and your work continues without you being there.[67]

Patrick Lencioni has written several wonderful books that have helped me throughout my career. One of his recent books, *The 6 Types of Working Genius*, helps you identify what you are not only incredible at doing but also what skills and talents give you energy versus take energy away. It's a great read!

Becoming a Thought Leader: The Ultimate Brand!

A thought leader is someone whose views are seen as authoritative and influential. "A thought leader is someone who, based on their expertise and industry perspective, offers unique guidance, inspires innovation and influences others."[68]

As a thought leader, your expertise, insight, and a valuable perspective give credibility to your position. These attributes demonstrate that you have a deep level of subject matter expertise. If you become a thought leader or subject matter expert, you don't earn this qualification quickly or easily. Remember Malcolm Gladwell's ten thousand hours? It takes several years to qualify as a true thought leader. If you need further convincing, here are some of the benefits to putting in the time and effort to become a thought leader:[69]

- It qualifies you as a reliable source of insight and information that can successfully influence others.

- It boosts your industry presence and builds your brand.

- It establishes credibility in your field.

- It encourages you to focus on what you know best and look for opportunities to express it frequently.

- It offers unique guidance and inspires innovation.

- It encourages forward thinking.

I was fortunate to work alongside some amazingly smart people during my career, including many thought leaders. During my final years at Humana, when my team and I were working to develop a population health model, we all became thought leaders on the topic. We could serve as population health thought leaders because of our extensive research, both inside Humana and in the field. We became credible resources for educating and informing people about population health. It was thrilling to be asked to speak on panels alongside other experts in the field, because we were experts as well!

As an executive, thought leadership augments my abilities and credibility and reaffirms how I show up in my world.

What Do You Want to Be Known For?

This is a tough question for most people to ask themselves. They don't want to come across as a know-it-all or a braggadocio. But the truth is, sometimes you have to brag! Not in a prideful way but in a confident way. If you don't brag about yourself and don't have anybody else to brag about you, that's not a good thing. There is nothing wrong with pointing out your strengths and talents and skills. Never forget there are a million problems going on at any given time in the world that need people like you to step in with solutions. What you're working to do is to take your talents, skills, and gifts and be a solution to somebody else's problem. I can tell you from experience, that is the best feeling in the world!

For example, if you are really good at analytics, then where in your organization are there people struggling with what you could come in and so comfortably solve? If you are really good at finding energy in a market, then be known in your market and take your company brand with you. This is not bragging or boasting; it is coming to the rescue on an issue that you are beautifully gifted to help resolve. Doing so is another element of generosity, when you take your expertise and push it out there, asking, "Who could use my help?" That feels wonderful. Remember, it's easy to be part of the problem, but you want one of those who finds the solution. When that happens, others will brag for you!

Getting the Word Out

You're ready to be a thought leader. You're clear on what you want to be known for. But how do you get the word out that you are ready to step out?

This is where promotion comes in, and most people aren't good at self-promotion. Think about your social media outlets and connections. What are you posting? How does what you post influence others' view of you? Are there free or paid public speaking events on the topic that audiences could benefit from hearing from you, the budding thought leader?

Look at other thought leaders. Who can you endorse, and who can endorse you? Look for opportunities to stand in front of people and talk about your gifts, skills, knowledge, and experience in your area of thought leadership. Does your organization have network resource groups, or affinity groups, as some people call them? Being a leader within these or other organized groups will often give you a platform on which to stand in front of executive leaders. Those leaders watch you demonstrate skills in galvanizing your peers, setting goals, building a marketing plan, and so on. Look for opportunities that give you a platform to showcase yourself as a thought leader.

LOOK FOR "THREEFERS"

When I first took the leadership role of president at Humana, I contacted a former AT&T leader who had helped me build my brand within that huge organization. Larry Bell gave me sage advice: look for the energy in the community, and plant Humana's flag there. So, I looked at the landscape of where the energy around health was within Houston's healthcare community. It was clearly coming from the very large hospital systems, and they were part of my very important supply chain. How could I become part of that energy? How could I be part of the solution to Houston's healthcare challenges?

I did my research and found that there was positive and vibrant energy in the American Heart Association's Go Red for Women movement.[70] All those large hospital systems were very strong supporters of this movement. Again, I took sage advice from another executive leader in the community and became the chairperson for the campaign, which meant Humana's name was big and bold with a great solution to heart health for women. This meant that hospital systems recognized us as a solution to the healthcare challenges, not a detractor. It also aligned me with twenty other executive women in the Houston area who were also big supporters of Go Red for Women. We soon became friends and business partners, helping each other succeed while helping Humana succeed in that market. This was a triple play, a "threefer"! I gained lifelong business friends, elevated Humana's brand in the community, and helped women the world over recognize their unique challenges with heart health.

Had I just volunteered, nobody would have known my name or, more importantly, Humana's name. I had to take a bold step. I had to put myself on a platform in front of people. I had to reach out to people I did not know and say, "Will you join us in this quest to give women visibility into their own heart health?" It was a great opportunity for my brand, for Humana's brand, and for the American Heart Association brand.

Show Up Every Day, and Make a Positive Impact

As I've shared previously, my brand attributes include high positive energy, executive presence, and being very approachable. Showing up every day to make a positive impact and to make people's lives better just because I'm there directly correlates to my brand.

But showing up that way every day isn't always easy to do.

During your decades-long career, there will be days when you are facing your own personal struggles: family issues, marital issues, kid issues, etc. You've got to ask yourself, "How do I drop personal issues at the office door or show up to meetings in a positive way? How am I going to separate mentally and emotionally?"

Creating separation between your personal and work life takes a level of maturity. And one way to build that maturity is what I called the ability to compartmentalize in chapter 5. I'm a firm believer that you have to put things in a box when you walk through that door or appear on that screen for work. You must put that box just outside your peripheral vision. You owe it to everybody you lead, or are led by, to show up as your best self! Putting things in a box is unique to each individual, but here are some of the common ways that can help you:

- Remove distractions by writing them down and then putting that document away. In my world, I write down the things I need to do or say when I get home to attend to a difficult situation and then put it out of sight, knowing that I have to commit to addressing the issue at the end of the day.

- Maintain boundaries by not taking calls/text messages that can upset you. In my world, I might tell myself, *At ten o'clock, I'm going to open that box at noon and give it ten minutes of my time, and then I'm going to put it away again.* Focus, focus, focus. Focus is a mental decision we make in the moment, because we all have the ability to choose what we think about.

- Have a fixed schedule that keeps you on track.

- If you find yourself back in a distracted state, allow yourself time to relax by doing some breathing exercises, taking a few moments to pray or meditate, or taking a walk around your office (ideally outside).

- Separate your emotions by identifying what is pertinent based on what you are called to do, right now. We all get caught between work and family demands. But right now, you are going into a meeting that you're excited about. How can you separate these two events in your mind?

At work, you owe it to the people you are around to give, not take, the energy from the room. Everyone is walking around with something, and you can be an island of sanity for others. Doing so just might make your situation seem more manageable.

Years ago, I had a family member who was an alcoholic. Many times, I would get phone calls in the middle of a workday, either from this person or from another relative saying, "We've got to do something!"

We? I couldn't do anything at that moment, so I stopped taking personal calls at work. I needed to stop the emotional drain I was feeling. I would tell myself, *At five, on my way home, I will give myself permission to think of ways I might be able to help, including empathizing with other relatives who feel helpless. I will prioritize dealing with this after I am done with my workday.* This didn't always work—there were repeated calls I eventually had to answer—but I tried to have a plan for dealing with this very difficult, sad, and distracting situation.

Not bringing my own problems and drama to work has greatly helped me throughout my career. I have been hypervigilant about this, but I have also developed great work friends whom I could turn to when I needed an outlet, even during the workday. When I think of the people who have hit a ceiling and gone no further, many times they were those who have brought drama to work. I've also known of many people who have handicapped their careers because they have perpetually brought outside issues into the workplace. My advice? Just don't do it.

Pattie Dale's Pertinent Points

- Your personal brand is what you stand for, what you are known for. It is the ongoing culmination of the experiences, skills, and values that differentiate you from those around you.

- Your professional life is a continual process of selling yourself. Whether you're in a job interview, interviewing for a promotion, or wanting to coach or mentor others, your job is to convince people you are the right person. This starts with your brand—what you are known for.

- Your transferable skills are part of your personal brand. You're going to meet people, you're going to build your network, you're going to use your leadership skills, all of which can be tapped into at your workplace.

- If you don't brag about yourself and don't have anybody else to brag about you, that's not a good thing. There is nothing wrong with pointing out your strengths, talents, and skills.

- Look for "threefers," which are times when you can benefit from something in three different ways.

- Creating separation between your personal and work life takes a level of maturity. One way to build that maturity is "the ability to compartmentalize."

CHAPTER 8

Be Ready for the Breaks

I learned so much from you about business, life, family, and faith, and especially to always remember the needs of others.

—DEDICATED TO MY DAD, J. Y. WILSON

M y dad, J. Y. Wilson, had a huge influence on my life, and I am much like him today. A World War II veteran, he was raised during the Great Depression, 1929–1939, and he learned to appreciate even the smallest of things because of the scarcity he witnessed as a young boy. I've always known him to be patient with me and to have a quiet strength that looked past the current circumstances to see the bigger picture. He was also the one who taught me to be ready for the breaks, because "they will surely come."

I can still remember being twenty-two and starting my first job at Mutual of New York, feeling a gamut of emotions with a trainload of thoughts running through my head. Excitement and anxiety. Hope and doubt.

Will I be good enough? Will I succeed? I don't know what I don't know, so can I know what's expected of me?

I was fortunate to have my dad's steady hand and guidance to lean upon during those early months. Every day when we talked, he would ask me, "How is your business?" He genuinely wanted to know and wanted to help me in any way. But the fact of the matter was that I would be the one to take my own journey, and I would be the one to make my own way through life. That can feel like a lonely, scary place, especially when you are stepping into your career journey for the very first time.

Whether you're starting your career, looking to reenter the workforce after a prolonged absence, or are a seasoned professional looking to give back, doubt and fear will try to creep into your mind and try to gain control over you. You're in a new place and a new stage of life. You may have family and friends to support you. You may have career advisors who have given you guidance.

But suddenly you're in this place called "work," and no one can do that work for you. You're on your own, perhaps for the first time. Income is restricted, but bills keep coming. The work at your place of employment is hard, but no one is going to do it for you. There is an excitement about the new, but the "What ifs?" are there as well. *What if I don't do a good enough job? What if someone asks me to do something I know nothing about?* Let me reassure you: this is all normal, and I promise you that you will get through this season!

I vividly remember my early days as an agent for Mutual of New York. All these "What ifs?" were whirling around in my mind. All these doubts about my ability were creeping into my psyche. I remember going to my childhood home one weekend and lamenting about all these pressures to my dad while he made breakfast. I explained that I was getting up early every morning to get a jump start on my workday, that I was working much more than I ever had before. But would it be enough? This wasn't like college or even high school, which had come fairly easily for me. After listening for several minutes, my dad, who was at the stove, looked over his shoulder, smiled, and said, "You've just got to put in the time." His words have stayed with me to this day, and I share the same words with others who come to me for mentoring, guidance, or just some advice.

Putting In the Time

The phrase *putting in the time* means being willing to sacrifice something in the short term to benefit you in the long run. You have to be willing to dedicate a certain amount of your time and make a special effort toward something specific. If you want to get in shape, you have to put time into exercising. If you want to learn something new, you have to put time into studying. If you want a promotion at work, you have to put time into learning new skills and delivering on your work to be done. In fact, in any area of life, there is no getting around putting in the time if you want to get ahead. Remember the earlier reference to Malcolm Gladwell's ten thousand hours to become an expert—that is putting in the time.

There is another side to putting in the time that is rarely given much attention: how you show up. This refers to how you walk into work each and every day, physically and mentally.

PHYSICALLY

The old saying, "You don't get a second chance to make a first impression" certainly applies to the way you show up for your career. Clothing choices for the workday have certainly changed since the pandemic, and it can be rather confusing to understand what is acceptable. While every organization and place of employment has its own dress code, the way people interpret the code can differ widely.

My advice is to take a cue from those you look up to in the workplace and consider adopting their dress code (assuming it adheres to the written policy in most aspects). During the early part of my career, formal business attire was the only acceptable attire in the workplace, such as suits and ties for men and suits or dresses (with sleeves!) for women. But in our post-COVID-19 world, with working from home being much more prevalent, people dress much less formally.

One interesting dress code I've recently encountered was called "dress for the day." That means if you are meeting with an outside client, going to court to try a case, or welcoming leadership from HQ, you would dial it up to a more formal look. On the days those big events weren't occurring, "dress for the day" means that business casual was just fine. Always remember that you never know when that break is coming. So, before you head out to work on any given day, ask yourself, *If something big were to happen, am I dressed for the moment?* Here's a tip: if casual dress is your norm, then keep something more formal handy so you can do a quick change when necessary. When you dress for success, you'll be physically prepared for the break that comes your way.

MENTALLY

In chapter 7, I talked about the need to compartmentalize your personal and professional life. This is part of putting in the time, and doing so will help you be prepared for the breaks that will inevitably come your way.

From day one of my career, I've shown up mentally with a positive attitude, with lots of energy, and with the ability to go in and get the task done. It was never enough just to show up "looking" like I had it together; I had to be prepared mentally to give my best. Granted, everyone has good and bad days. However, I know from experience that maintaining a positive attitude is a *choice* we make. A positive attitude affects our well-being, our job performance, and our job satisfaction. I've learned to include practical things such as being around optimistic people and reading positive content. I've also learned that using positive language versus negative language and managing my choice of words helps me maintain a good mental attitude.

Other tips to help maintain a healthy attitude include the following:

- Keep to daily routines if you're a person who likes consistency, or incorporate the new if you like more excitement.

- Foster kindness whenever possible.

- Be a curious person, and always look to learn something new.

- Practice deep breathing whenever anxiety tries to creep in.

- Create high points—things you can look forward to—each day and week.

- Assume responsibility—when it is yours—and decide what your response and reaction will be ahead of time.

- Have a personal mission statement that you live by and goals that you want to reach recorded in some place accessible; review whenever you need to.

- No one owes you anything, so stop complaining, stop blaming, and eliminate the victim mentality. It is not a good reflection of who you are.

- See the good and minimize the bad. As the old saying goes, in every dark cloud, there is a silver lining.

- Keep the long term in mind, and remember that career life is a marathon, not a sprint.

I can guarantee you two things: 1) If you *don't* put in the time, the breaks you are looking for will never happen. 2) If you *do* put in the time, you will be ready when the breaks come. Always remember that when you put in the time, you will be prepared to be in the right place at the right time to take advantage of whatever comes your way.

Preparing Myself for the Breaks

When I received my first promotion at AT&T, it meant a move from our current home in Jacksonville, Florida, to the work location in Cincinnati, Ohio. At the same time, Jim Tye was working hard on his career, and the opportunity to go to Orlando to build out his own company came his way. We had a big decision to make: Do we continue living in the same house and have one or both of us look for another break? Or would we live separately during the week so that we could take advantage of *both* career opportunities?

We chose the latter, and that was the pattern we followed for eight years, with Jim Tye taking weekend trips to visit me wherever I might have landed. (The good furniture and the cats always came with me!) Yes, this was a sacrifice, but one that we were both prepared to make, with the words of my dad echoing in our heads: "When the breaks come, you need to be able to take them."

This eight-year period not only propelled our careers; it also enhanced our marriage. We were fully supportive of each other, and we learned quickly to take full advantage of our precious time together. We also learned to plan ahead and purchased months' worth of airline tickets for the weekend trips to reunite. We never missed a weekend, and it was a wonderful time for our marriage.

This eight-year period also taught us to be prepared that the next break might come at any time. My second big break came when I had the opportunity to work for a dynamic SVP—sales vice president—in Washington, DC. I remember Jim Tye and I going out for dinner to discuss this move and then looking at each other and saying, "We can do this!" Ultimately, he joined me in Washington, DC, and we had a fabulous time together. This then led to another break and another set of relocations. And so on and so on.

My favorite move was to AT&T's headquarters in New Jersey. As it turned out, Jim Tye's next big break took him to New Jersey, too, and our work locations were so close together that for the first time in years we could actually have lunch together! I followed my dad's advice, as did Jim Tye: we kept our parallel careers moving forward and maintained a strong and growing marriage. And I can tell you for certain that God kept his powerful hand in our lives the entire time! Still does!

A "PERSONAL BREAK"

On Valentine's Day 1999, after another big career break, I had relocated again and was staying alone in a corporate apartment in Houston, Texas. At about seven in the evening, there was a knock on the door, and when I opened it, a delivery person was waiting with two dozen roses! Jim Tye had always sent me boxed roses on Valentine's Day, and he had once again found a way to do so all the way from his current big break location—San Francisco. There was a note attached written in his left-handed slant telling his landlord that he no longer needed his apartment and would be moving to Houston to be with his wife! I still have that letter, and it is precious to me. From that day on, we decided to take advantage of a "personal break" that came our way. From that day on, we agreed to never live apart again. And we never have!

I can confidently tell you that from day one, Jim Tye and I never put our careers over our marriage, but we certainly made sure our marriage accommodated our careers. We had to do a lot of meaningful planning, and doing so allowed us both to take advantage of the breaks that came our way.

You Don't Have to Have It All Together

In our early days, Jim Tye and I followed a very nontraditional marriage given how much time we spent apart. But in today's world, the nontraditional has become the traditional, and whatever works for two people ... well, that's what works for them. And when it comes to your career path, it may look anything but traditional! However, one thing will always remain the same: in life and in career, moving forward means having to face the unknown.

The unknown can bring with it a real sense of intimidation. There's a scariness factor. So, how do you come up with the courage to walk through a door, not really knowing what's on the other side? Here are a few things that have helped me alleviate fear and anxiety:

- Connecting

  No matter what you're about to do or what career move you're about to embark on, you will interact with people, and doing so means establishing relationships. From the outset, I always try to appreciate the individuals I'm connecting with. I also look for areas in which we have commonality and where our values match.

- No perfection needed

  We women tend to want everything to be perfect, and we want ourselves to be perfect as well! But career opportunities don't require that you have *all* the capabilities and competencies required for a role. I've learned that if I have three-quarters of what is necessary, I will build out a team that helps me get the rest of what is needed. Whenever I'm making a decision about a particular role, I'm looking for two things: 1) affirmation from God that I'm going in the right direction, and 2) affirmation from my husband through his objective point of view. A lot of prayer goes into making those decisions. But if I have that value map, if I feel that this is God's plan and my husband looks me in the eyes and says, "You can do this!" then the decision is no longer scary but exciting!

  In your case, perhaps you have someone you've worked for or a former leader whom you can count on to give you solid input. Maybe you have a trusted friend or a parent to whom you can talk. Explain why you think you would be a good fit for this role, and tell them about the company's values and its missions. Talk to them about the people you will be working with and the leader you're going to work for. Make sure theirs is a strong values match. The person you go to should be a good listener with an objective mindset, someone who has your best interests at heart.

- Let people see you at your best

  In a corporate or organizational environment, assume that you are always being watched and evaluated and the way you present yourself is of utmost importance. If you want to grow your career, then what they see needs to be your best. If you are having a rough day, if you are the type of person who wears your heart on your sleeve, make it a point to be less visible that day. Be remembered as the person who is positive and a forward thinker. You don't need to wear a fake smile or be the constant cheerleader; instead, find ways to make a positive impact. That might mean volunteering for the next assignment rather than waiting for it to come to you. It means taking on the challenging work rather than trying to duck out.

  When you're asked to lead, when you step up and volunteer to be the one who hosts or facilitates a holiday event, show up as your best and turn that opportunity into a break, because somebody's watching you organizing, leading, and working with your team. I'm not suggesting that you volunteer for everything that comes your way. Go back to what lights you up, which can give you a map to opportunities that are not necessarily in your current career path or your workday. For instance, if you love planning events, join your network resource group and take a leadership role. Take ownership for a task, which just might lead to a break for you. You suddenly have a platform, and you're in front of leaders or managers whom you don't normally stand before.

They may be looking for people just like you to move to the next rung. Be ready to show up at your best!

- Be prepared

    You can't just show up at a meeting—you need to show up well prepared with your research completed and in hand, ready to present. For example, I'll read press releases, review organizational charts, and learn all I can about the people attending the meeting and what their value is to the company or organization. I'll flip through pertinent books and current news articles. I'll scan several news outlets and newsletters I receive daily, such as the *Wall Street Journal*, the *New York Times*, *Harvard Business Review*, McKinsey, and *The Morning Brew*, and I'll check out X, which was formerly Twitter. Then I ask myself, *What information, value, experience, and/or skills can I contribute? How can I bring new knowledge and insights? What can I do to create, recreate, or strengthen what already exists?*

    Try to anticipate any surprises that might crop up and what you'll do if that happens. If something comes up that you're not prepared for, instead of feeling embarrassed and scrambling for an answer, say something like "That's a great question; let me get back to you on that."

    Take a lesson from me. There have been times when I've worked hard to get invited to a meeting. But when I showed up, I was in the uncomfortable position of not being fully prepared, and it was obvious to all that others were more prepared than me. And when I'm at a table of smart people, it's important that I have something to say that adds value. So, I had to sit quietly and not say anything. I could have beaten myself up in the aftermath; instead, I owned the fact that I wasn't prepared and used it as a catalyst to do better going forward. I learned not to do myself the disservice of just showing up without being fully prepared.

My father always told me to be ready because the breaks would come, and he cautioned me to be ready when they came my way. I trained myself to watch for them, not to discount anything without an evaluation, and to avoid saying no to these opportunities. When the phone call came or the new opportunity presented itself, I put it through my "filter" (more on that later) and tried to say, "Yes!"

Many times, I was surprised that the opportunity someone presented seemed out of my skill or experience level. But the person on the other side knew more than I did, and they believed I could succeed in the role even though I didn't appear to have all the components that would comprise the "right" background. This will repeatedly happen in your career, too. You'll be shocked when they want you to do something, because you think you don't know how to do it. Others see something in you that you're not able to see at that moment.

- Take credit

  I'm sure you've heard the saying, "Give credit where credit is due." That applies to giving yourself credit as well! I'm not saying be braggadocious or egotistical. I am saying be brave and confident enough to own what you've done and the benefits it's brought to your organization.

  Years ago, while I was at AT&T, my talented mentor, Larry Bell, presented me with an opportunity to sit in front of a group of vice presidents and present my work. Doing so was certainly nerve wracking, but I was able to comfortably own what I had done and talk about the changes I had made to a very important process. It was a beautiful process, but it also had flaws, so I redrafted the process and built it to be stronger and more sustainable. At the end of the meeting, I knew I had landed it, and when I looked over at Larry, I could see he was very proud. When we were wrapping up, one of the vice presidents asked when I could make this same presentation to his leadership team. That was a success! And a happy dance moment!

If you have a strong sense of grace and humility, I understand that it can be hard to take credit. For humble people, this is a place of discomfort. But remind yourself that you aren't taking credit away from someone else. You are being authentic about the work you've done or the team you've led while giving credit where credit is due to others. If you assembled the team and you're pulling the team to the place of being able to deliver the work or a great product, it's okay to say that. This was *your* team. You looked at the skills needed to put this across the finish line, and you gathered your team together and led them to this place. Yes, your team is full of very smart, talented people, and you are blessed to lead them. Take credit—not away from someone else, but for what is due to you.

- Have confidence

  To me, confidence is having the ability to walk into a room full of strangers, hold back my shoulders, and comfortably say, "Hi, I'm Pattie Dale Tye." Confidence grows with increased knowledge, understanding, and experience. I'm at a point where I'm confident in myself and can take the lead in areas I might not know a lot about or even truly know what

I'm doing. Why? Because I have confidence in who I am and in my abilities. I also know how to surround myself with others whom I can team with so we can get the job done.

Give Someone Else a Break!

Whether you are starting out, reentering the workforce, or serving others as a seasoned professional, to someone else you are "all grown up and the big leader." No matter your position, no matter your title, remember that you are where you are because of the breaks you've received. So, be on the lookout for opportunities to give someone else a break! You see someone who has confidence but lacks experience. You know someone who has knowledge but lacks confidence. In other words, you see *potential*. Pair that potential with a break!

When I was the COO of ChaseCom in Houston, I needed to replace a key position, the vice president of my contact center. I interviewed several highly qualified people, but there was one who, while not having all the experience the role needed, really stood out in the crowd of applicants. Morgan Smith was the standout, and I felt he just needed a platform from which to excel, a place to grow his leadership skills and talents. And excel he did! He gave us all he had, and then he went on to his next great position.

While I had the final say in hiring, my senior vice president and I saw great potential in Morgan. He may not have had all the skills and experience that would have been optimal, so we knew we would have to weave our hands together and say, "Step here." He took the steps we offered and served the firm beautifully until he outgrew us. He was a great leader and left us far better than when he arrived.

When giving someone else a break, you are not looking for someone who has 100 percent of what you need. They may have 60 percent, and the team around them can provide 40 percent. And if this is truly the right person for the job, they will grow into what the role fully needs. This is exactly what other people did for me. They knew I didn't have everything; I wasn't the perfect candidate, but I was the *right* one. They saw potential in me and afforded me every opportunity to grow, personally and professionally, because of what they saw *in* me.

Conclusion

I'm a curious person with high energy, and I'm eager to jump in to something new. I can honestly say that I have gained a PhD in learning through the "classroom of career" without ever going to those PhD classes. I can look back on my career and be so thankful that I really have not missed much.

My career path has taken me into ten different industries in nine different cities with dozens of leaders. To say the least, I've had a very diverse career, and all that I learned and loved at each different stage or city, I've taken into the next new market or role.

Diversification has given me a million squares on my career quilt. I can look at each one of them and be grateful for the experience and thankful for the people I've worked with and the friends I've gained. Diversification in my career and life also led me to Jim Tye and a fabulous thirty-three-year marriage. If I hadn't taken the breaks that came my way, I would have missed out on so much! Health, faith, family, and career are all gifts, and diversification is key to treasuring each one.

Preparation is key to helping you be ready for the breaks that come your way. And those breaks are both personal and divine. They are personal because you have to put in the time, you have to do the work, and you have to be prepared. They are divine because breaks often come out of the blue and when you least expect them. But when those divine incidences happen, you will have the confidence to show up and walk through the door of opportunity … as long as you have put in the time, done the work, and have prepared yourself!

Pattie Dale's Pertinent Points

- Whether you're starting your career, looking to reenter the workforce after a prolonged absence, or in the third stage and looking to give back, doubt and fear will try to creep into your mind and try to gain control over you. Let me reassure you: this is all normal, and I promise you that you will get through this season!
- Make my dad's words, "You've got to put in the time," one of your mantras.
- Review the bulleted list introduced by the line "Other tips to help maintain a healthy attitude include the following"; think about what you can include that you know will work for you.
- In a corporate or organizational environment, assume that you are always being watched and evaluated and that the way you present yourself is of utmost importance. If you want to grow your career, what they see needs to be your best.
- Remind yourself that you aren't taking credit away from someone else. You are being authentic about the work you've done or the team you've led while giving credit where credit is due to others.
- No matter your position, no matter your title, remember that you are where you are because of the breaks you've received. So, be on the lookout for opportunities to give someone else a break! You see someone who has confidence but lacks experience. You know someone who has knowledge but lacks confidence. In other words, you see *potential*.

CHAPTER 9

Look at You Now

You taught me the meaning of "lifting while you climb, giving back to go forward, and the importance of leaving a legacy."
—DEDICATED TO TONY CHASE

C ast your eyes forward ten to twenty years, and imagine living into the excitement of the statement, "Look at you now!" You've done it! You've had an amazingly success-ful career. What is outside your castle window? (Recall the book *Forget a Mentor, Find a Sponsor: The New Way to Fast-Track Your Career*, by Sylvia Ann Hewlett, and the view from my window described in chapter 2). What do you see outside your office window on the last day of your career? Who has helped you along the journey, and whom have you helped? What is the legacy you are leaving in the work world, or the entire world?

Tony Chase, the former CEO at ChaseCom, taught me the notion of lifting while you climb. *Lifting while you climb* means that you take someone with you on the journey, someone who needs your help. Tony also lived by the adage, "Do well by doing good." Tony lifted while he climbed, and he still does! Tony also taught me to do my work as if it would be my legacy work. Tony gave me my first break when he took a chance on hiring me. He stressed the fact that everything I do, every single day, will impact someone else, negatively or positively, and the impact of my work would be the building of my legacy.

When I was first hired to be the COO at ChaseCom, the company was in its start-up phase. We were a small leadership team, and the days and nights were long, with all of us rolling up our sleeves to get everything done. When our energy started to wane, when our moods began to shift, Tony would say, "Stop and take a deep breath. Now, think about what type of impact you want your work to have, and think about the legacy you want to leave while doing that work."

Often, we would take out a pen and notebook and write out what we wanted to be remembered for. What did we want to leave behind when we moved on to our next role? What did we want people to say about us once this company had grown into its full body? Immediately, energy blew into the room and we were back on track. That energy also reminded us that we weren't doing what we *had* to do; we were doing what we *wanted* to do! And what we were doing wasn't just about us; it was about whom we were going to impact. We were a team again. We had our eyes looking in the right direction, our ears listening for the aha moments, and our work blossomed again.

• • • • •

No matter what you do, no matter how much you enjoy your work, there will be times when you'll simply get tired. You might get tired of the hours you're putting in. You might get tired of the routine. You might get tired of having to innovate or find new customers. In fact, there are times when you will get downright exhausted! It's easy to ride the energy wave when things are going well. But when you're tired—and even more so when you're exhausted—it's vital that you take some time to breathe. Whether you're leading a team or part of a team, you need to take some time to stop and take a look at what you're doing and where you want to go. Take a look at the big picture to see what impact you are making and what legacy you are leaving. Remind yourself that what you are doing isn't just for your benefit.

Servant Leadership

You've probably heard the term *servant leadership*, but perhaps you've never thought about the positive impact it can have on your workplace and the work relationships you have.

The term *servant leadership* was coined by Robert K. Greenleaf in an essay he first published in 1970 titled "The Servant as Leader," noting the following:

> A servant-leader focuses primarily on the growth and well-being of people and the communities to which they belong. While traditional leadership generally involves the accumulation and exercise of power by one at the "top of the pyramid," servant leadership is different. The servant-leader shares power, puts the needs of others first and helps people develop and perform as highly as possible.[71]

The Society of Human Resource Management Executive Network states that "servant leadership is a leadership style that prioritizes the growth, well-being, and empowerment of employees. It aims to foster an inclusive environment that enables everyone in the organization to thrive as their authentic self."[72]

I worked many years as a servant leader without knowing the term even existed. I simply knew that remembering the needs of others was part of my DNA, at work and in the wide world.

Confidence and Generosity Go Hand in Hand

Showing confidence in your ability to do the work needed to be done and doing it with generosity in service to others, not just yourself, makes life much easier and rewarding. Taking these traits into the workplace has enabled me to have a fulfilling, successful career, ultimately holding the role of an engaging, impactful leader while positively impacting those I have been fortunate enough to serve alongside.

Granted, it's not always easy to embody confidence, and it can be hard to see how generosity or serving others versus serving self ladders up to success in the workplace. But I can unequivocally tell you that my career is illustrative of how these critical traits can open doors of opportunity and present breaks that you would never have thought possible.

During my time as Humana's market president in Houston, I made it a point to engage with each and every one of our employees at least once a week. I felt I needed to allow them an unfiltered opportunity to speak with me about whatever was on their mind. Were they being held back by any barriers that I could remove? Were there work pressures I wasn't aware of that I could remediate? How were they doing personally? What were they celebrating or feeling saddened by? My method for this engagement was to wheel around a cart of fresh fruit and share with each individual, listening and learning. My dear and fabulous assistant, Angie LaBove, always made sure this precious time was blocked off in my calendar every week. And she also made sure there was plenty of fruit. I treasured that time and those conversations with folks who may not have comfortably come into my office just to talk.

CONFIDENCE IN YOURSELF

There are times when confidence fuels your drive and enthusiasm to move forward. And there are times when your confidence will be chipped away at and people, events, and/or circumstances align against you. But if you can be *intentional* about remaining confident, even when life temporarily colludes against you, you don't have to cave in, and you can choose to continue moving forward.

Both my parents modeled a healthy sense of confidence without being braggadocios. Instead, they radiated trustworthiness and approachability. Even in his last years, my father, through the fog of dementia, never lost his strong, confident stance nor his commitment to caring for others. I remember watching him walk through the halls of the hospital or memory care ward, stopping to greet everyone and helping anyone who needed it. I am so grateful my parents showed me the value of confidence and approachability. Both traits are both deeply ingrained in me today ... and I see them in my siblings as well.

Confidence in the workplace is feeling capable of doing the work you've been tasked with. This doesn't mean you walk in on day one being 100 percent capable of doing everything. But remember, you were hired because someone viewed your history—in school or the workplace—and concluded that you could perform the work. With that thought as your foundation, you can begin to move forward, do what you can, ask for guidance when you need it, and then continue moving forward. Slowly, your history will connect with the current work requirements and your capabilities will grow, as will your confidence.

CONFIDENCE STARTS WITH SELF-DISCOVERY

Understanding your talents and interests is essential. You're not just your degree or profession, and you have much to offer. Understanding where and how your abilities and interests align with your career will help you determine a specific field where you can bloom. You may not immediately connect your natural talents and capabilities with your confidence, but the more you develop your talents and capabilities, the more confident you become.

My early career in insurance

- piqued my interest by tapping into my natural skills in analytics and service;

- opened doors to a successful career at AT&T; and

- thirty years later, led to my landing an extraordinary opportunity with one of the nation's largest insurers, Humana.

I often think about the aptitude-testing experience, because you can't fight your natural tendencies. Even when I knew nothing about actuarial science, my natural analytical tendencies helped me become a leader in that space.

Discover your natural talents by

- taking an online assessment;

- seeking people and places to help you discover your talents; and

- exploring how your talents and skills might apply to a variety of industries.

OWNING YOUR PLACE AT THE TABLE

Having confidence allows you to show up graciously, humbly, and prepared.

There are two kinds of confidence: good and arrogant. The good kind of confidence makes you very approachable, and approachability is a big factor in career success. I mention this because overly confident or arrogantly confident people often put up a fence around themselves, making them unapproachable. If leaders, team members, clients, and partners don't feel they can approach you with issues, news, problems, or solutions, you'll miss many opportunities for course correction and guidance, and you'll be left out of crucial conversations (a career nonstarter).

At all costs, avoid falling into the trap of being arrogantly confident. Doing so can fool you into thinking you have to have all the answers or tell you that you are the smartest person in the room. The best leaders I've encountered during my career have comfortably acknowledged they didn't know it all and needed a team around them whose collective intelligence would be far superior to their own.

55/38/7 FORMULA

A young woman who used to work for me was very good at her job. Yet she appeared to be unsure of herself. Whenever we talked, she covered half her face with her hands. One day, I asked her to try to speak with her hands folded in her lap. She struggled at first but ultimately made it through our conversation. Afterward, she asked why I made her do that. I told her, "If you're covering your face or hunched over, you appear to lack confidence. If you're fidgeting, it makes people wonder why, or it may lead them to question whether you are hiding something. You are a bright and very talented person; don't dilute those special qualities through body language."

Albert Mehrabian is professor emeritus of psychology at the University of California, Los Angeles, best known for his study of body language and communication. He found the following:[73]

- The bulk, 55 percent, of communication is translated by body language.

- A significant 38 percent of how we're perceived comes from how we speak (tone of voice and inflection).

- Only 7 percent of our message comes from what we actually say.

Body language that sends the wrong signals can be a tricky habit to break. We're not always conscious of our posture, facial expressions, fidgeting, personal space, or hand gestures. You could try recording yourself, but we often are so accustomed to our mannerisms that it can be hard to assess ourselves. Instead, asking others for feedback is the best way to find out how our body language and tone of voice come across. Another great trick is watching and then mirroring others who exhibit good confidence, body language, tone of voice, and inflection. Challenge yourself to stand or sit straighter, talk loud enough to be heard across the table, and be mindful of fidgeting.

Not only does posture show confidence and capability to others, but researchers at Ohio State University found that the simple act of sitting up straight increases our self-image simultaneously.[74] Work on it, and notice how your self-esteem and self-worth increase each time you do.

KEEP GETTING BACK UP

Think back to when you were learning to walk. You certainly fell multiple times, but you didn't let that keep you down (literally and figuratively). Learning any new skill and having the confidence to put it into practice entails taking risks and being willing to fall down. Getting back up is the hard part. But that's where growth and resilience develop.

Cultivating Confidence at Work

EARLY CAREER

It's time to take stock of what makes you unique and valuable, giving you confidence in who you are right *now*, so you can remain confident as you build your fabulous career. Start with the same list you had when applying to college or university and continually refresh it. Ask your parents, friends, and professors how they would describe your accomplishments and skills. Build on your uniqueness, refine it, hone it, and read it in front of the mirror often. Find the thread that makes you successful. Write it down and say it aloud. It may change over time, but you need to know and own it to tell others who you are and why you should be on or leading the team.

MIDCAREER AND RETURNING WORKERS

Take time to remember all you have learned and accomplished. Spend some quiet time mining all your memories and experiences. No one knows you better than you. If you can't easily list them, you won't be able to share them. I challenge you to write them down, read them aloud, and douse yourself in confidence; you are unique and valuable. There's a career match for all you bring to the table.

LEADERS

When employees are called in to the leader's office, they're often full of dread. (We're conditioned to think that whoever has power also judges us, often negatively.) People work best when they feel supported, heard, and acknowledged. As a leader, your success should depend on your employees' success, so do everything you can to help them show up at their best. Make yourself approachable and available.

I recall my first meeting with Gail McGovern, then president at AT&T and now the American Red Cross CEO. Gail didn't sit behind her enormous desk during our meeting; she sat in a chair beside me. That small gesture made the meeting so much more comfortable and productive. From that day forward, I tried never to sit behind my desk during meetings, nor at the head of the table.

• • • • •

At any stage of your career, do the following:

- Keep an "I value myself" folder on your computer (or in a binder) with positive feedback from coworkers, teachers, and family members or comments from a stranger. Refer back to it when you need a pick-me-up.

- Recognize the warning signs that imposter syndrome is coming to visit, and be proactive in locking the door.

- Forget about those who have tried to negate you; instead, focus on your strengths.

- Talk with a career counselor or your leader to create an action plan for using what you excel at to strengthen your weaker spots.

- Decide where you want to put your energy, and do what lights you up.

- Keep your eyes open for opportunities (you can wave these in imposter syndrome's face).

Generosity: Supporting Yourself and Others at the Table

There is no end to generosity. It creates a beautiful circle of lifting the lives of others, who continue to lift others as well. Countless people have helped me throughout my career, from my early days as a furniture manufacturer's rep to my senior leadership role at Humana. They took chances on me and put me in bigger and better places, and

I can't imagine not helping others. In return, my ask of others I help is that they do the same for someone else.

Don't forget to be generous with yourself as well, as noted in chapter 1. When you can't fill your own cup, you feel a sense of scarcity and don't see what you have to give to others.

Be willing to take the gifts you are given along the way—especially advice from people and mentors when you are new in your career or new to a role. Be open. Listen. Allow others to generously help you get where you need to go. This is what happened during my time in the furniture industry.

When I was a new rep in the furniture business, I met the wonderful owner of a great furniture store in my territory. He watched me stutter and stammer during my first pitch; then he took the time to take me under his wing, saying, "Let me show you how to do this." Our collective business grew exponentially, thanks to the generosity of time and energy of this kind man and his employees. I'll never forget Damon Casemore's kindness, and I'm constantly on the lookout for ways I can help others as he helped me. This reciprocal generosity keeps the wheel moving, and I believe it makes the world a better place!

GENEROSITY IN YOUR COMMUNITY

In every phase of your career, you will be part of many communities, including your team, company division, company headquarters, and local organizations where you work, live, and play. Be the one who helps others by sharing the wealth of generosity to improve the community around you.

Generosity can be as simple as giving compliments and boosting the confidence of others, letting them know you think they can accomplish a particular task. Right now, someone is scared to death of giving a presentation or doubting their ability to make a difference at work. One supportive statement from you could remove the butterflies that could cause them to stumble and fail. This costs you nothing, but the return is huge!

Be an active participant in the community around you. Put yourself forward, and engage in the various programs your employer has made available to you: network resource groups, volunteer days and events, celebrations, and activities for charitable causes. Be the one who shows up and offers to help organize or promote the next event or drive. This will help you stand out, make you feel great, and help you to be an important part of your community.

When I was promoted to Humana's headquarters in Louisville, it seemed huge! With its thousands of employees, I didn't want to just blend into the crowd; I wanted to find a way to stand out in a positive way. When the opportunity to cochair Humana's annual United Way campaign came my way, I jumped at it! During my first ninety days in this massive HQ location, this volunteer opportunity gave me the break to speak with Humana's most senior leaders about something near and dear to my heart: giving back. This opportunity also gave me a platform to speak to thousands of my fellow employees. All in all, it was a "threefer." I gave back to the community, I was given a voice, and I had a face to my voice. I have always been passionate about the United Way, and it was a beautiful thing to come into this new community and immediately be able to give back.

Two years later, that single volunteer opportunity turned into the career moment of a lifetime. Our company embarked on an entirely new way of supporting health in communities, and my name was associated with giving back in communities. I was asked to lead this exciting new initiative, and I was able to be extremely generous in communities that needed generosity the most.

Trust me on this: generosity will always help you ladder up! You can never go wrong with being generous. It's truly a gift that will give back again and again.

GENEROSITY IN THE FACE OF SCARCITY

What happens to generosity when scarcity arrives? There will be times when your team, department, business, or organization will need to cut back on resources. It's the ebb and flow of our work world. Be careful with how you react in those times. Sadly, when scarcity of resources arrives on the doorstep, you may witness how dysfunctional a team, project, or company can become.

People may hide information, hoard ideas, step on one another's toes to get their fair share, etc. Being privy to this can really chip away at your confidence and even cause you to not share ideas, to be less kind and generous to team members, and to limit your willingness to help others. You may begin to doubt your worth and forget all those great attributes that make you worthy of occupying the work space you've been given.

When you feel yourself entering into a scarcity mindset, get rid of it—quickly. Be intentional about keeping your confidence and generosity intact. Remind yourself that you have enough, that you are capable. You can accomplish much more when scarcity is no longer part of your vocabulary. Be your own champion of confidence and generosity during the inevitable ups and downs at work. When you do this, you'll fill your life with more treasure than even your paycheck could ever provide.

CULTIVATING GENEROSITY AT WORK

When you are first starting your career, I encourage you to give early and give often. Even small actions can lead to big changes, which can lead to breaks that you never thought possible. The generosity of one person brings together a constellation of seemingly insignificant events, which creates joy in the hearts of everyone who participates and/or receives. Nurture your relationships with generosity, and watch the doors of opportunity open before you!

If you're a seasoned professional or returning to work, you have received so much in your career already, meaning you have much to give. Even if you are new to a workplace or have entirely pivoted to a new profession, you are always at least one step ahead of someone else. Take that person or team under your wing. Offer support and freely give your time. Remain open to receiving from others, including your leaders. Never stop learning and growing! Flex your generosity muscle daily until it runs on autopilot.

LEADERS

In your role as a leader, your time is precious and often stretched thin. Are you making your team members' growth and development a priority? If not, it's time to reprioritize. None of us got to where we are by going it alone. We've had mentors and been mentors (even if we didn't realize it). Just because you're more seasoned doesn't mean you can't still benefit from a mentor or by being a mentor. Keep in mind that there are still many lessons to be learned, and some will come from those junior members of your team.

A Threefold Cord

Servant leadership, confidence, and generosity are gifts that are free to give and receive. They are like a threefold cord, which is not easily broken.[75] I couldn't feel as confident in myself without knowing that I am also generous in doing work that will benefit others through my servant leadership. When you are generous in the workplace, you will stand out. When you back up that standing out with confidence in your ability to do the work, breaks will come your way. And when you are a servant leader, your career will benefit deeply and quickly.

With this threefold cord you will

- be noticed;

- be needed and depended upon;

- learn;

- succeed; and

- enable others to succeed.

This threefold cord in the workplace embodies the concept that you aren't doing this just for yourself; you are working to make the life of someone else better. That person might be your leader, teammate, or the end user consumer of the product or service you've been hired to support. In this way, you are filling in many spaces the role you were hired to fill requires.

I'll wrap up with wise words from my father. He ended every meal's blessing with "Help us to always remember the needs of others." That is chiseled into my every fiber, and this mindset has been a career game changer. Helping others through servant leadership, being confident in my abilities, and being generous toward others has been impactful throughout my career in ways I cannot begin to count. If you do the same, the beautiful things you experience will never cease to amaze you!

154

Pattie Dale's Pertinent Points

- When your team's energy starts to wane, when their moods begin to shift, remind your team members to stop and take a deep breath. Then, think about what type of impact you want your work to have, and think about the legacy you want to leave while doing that work.

- Showing confidence in your ability to do the work needed and doing it with generosity in service to others, not just yourself, makes life much easier and rewarding.

- There are times when your confidence will be chipped away at and people, events, and/or circumstances align against you. But if you can be *intentional*—intentionality is a choice—about remaining confident, even when life temporarily colludes against you, you don't have to cave in, and you can choose to continue moving forward.

- If leaders, team members, clients, and partners don't feel they can approach you with issues, news, problems, or solutions, you'll miss many opportunities for course correction and guidance, and you'll be left out of crucial conversations (a career nonstarter).

- Experiences from setbacks and resulting imposter syndrome will happen during your career. Don't panic; you are not alone. Just remember, you control the reaction to every outcome—nobody else.

- Don't forget to be generous with yourself as well. When you can't fill your own cup, you feel a sense of scarcity and don't see what you have to give to others.

Find a way to say yes to things. Say yes to invitations to a new country, say yes to meet new friends, say yes to learn something new. Yes is how you get your first job, and your next job, and your spouse, and even your kids. Even if it's a bit edgy, a bit out of your comfort zone, saying yes means that you will do something new, meet someone new, and make a difference. Yes lets you stand out in a crowd, be the optimist, see the glass full, be the one everyone comes to. Yes is what keeps us all young.
—ERIC SCHMIDT, FORMER EXECUTIVE
CHAIRMAN OF GOOGLE

I want to sincerely thank you for being part of my career journey! Writing this book has given me the opportunity to give back what has so generously been given to me throughout my career! Taking a cue from Eric Schmidt, when I said yes to writing this book, I once again entered a new, uncharted territory, and I am profoundly thankful that you have journeyed along this new path with me. My hope for you, my new friends and readers, is that the time you've invested in this book will return to you tenfold in a great and successful career—and that you, too, will help others and be a positive influence in their lives. It's a beautiful legacy for me to think that there are people I may never see in a face-to-face environment who feel they've gotten to know me through my career journey … and that my journey might help them.

Writing this book has been a bit edgy for me—certainly a bit out of my comfort zone. But sharing the wisdom I've been fortunate enough to gain during my career really lights me up! I'm grateful for what God has allowed me to do in my life, and I'm passionate about the possibilities that await me, even now as a seasoned professional.

What about You?

I hope you'll keep in mind that every day you wake up, you have the opportunity to make a positive impact on someone's life, both personally and professionally. Don't treat lightly the impact you have on those you're walking through life with, and pay attention to the legacy you want to leave—especially during those lulls in life and the inevitable valleys you will go through.

During those times, remind yourself to roll up your sleeves and do the positive work you need to do, which will give you the energy to keep moving forward. And when you're on the mountaintop and everything is coming together, remember to stop, take a breath, and enjoy the moment. But also remind yourself that the work you are doing is not all about you; no matter what you are doing, there are others around you with whom to share the wealth—whatever that wealth looks like—whenever possible. Sharing that wealth means you are being generous, and generosity can show up in many ways, such as investment, wisdom, spirit, ideas, time, and relationships. So, be generous, and be generous often!

Your impact and legacy will also be hallmarked by your kindness and approachability. You'll be amazed how kindness and approachability lead to greater levels of confidence in yourself and your abilities. So, be a mentor. Be a sponsor. Step out of your comfort zone, and offer someone the encouragement they need—and want! As Gandhi said, "Be the change you want to see." And as Pattie Dale Tye says, "Be the leader you want to be led by!"

Recently, I had the privilege of helping a young woman determine if she needed to stay in her current role or take a risk and move into another one. We talked through all the pros and cons, looked three to five career steps out, and dug deeply into what her passions were and what lights her up. Finally, when her decision was to jump onto that next new role, we worked out a plan to leave her current role with respect and honor and join her new role standing as tall as she possibly could. I have no doubt she will have the confidence to help someone else do the same one day. That will be the beautiful completion of the circle of my career life: helping one who will help another, who will help another, who will help another.

Until our paths cross again, I pray for God's richest blessings over your life and much success throughout your career!

D r. Debra Clary has developed the following assessment tool that I've found to be a great help with my teams and developing the level of curiosity. Curiosity is a key trait that all people have to some degree, and in leadership and within teams, it can be a driving force for change at all levels.

The Curiosity Curve

The Curiosity Curve© is an assessment tool designed to measure and evaluate the level of curiosity within individuals, teams, and organizations. Curiosity is a valuable trait that can drive innovation, problem solving, and adaptability, leading to better business results, employee retention, and an enhanced customer experience.

By using the Curiosity Curve, organizations can assess and understand how curious their employees and teams are, which can help identify areas for improvement and development. It can be an effective tool for encouraging a culture of curiosity and fostering an environment where new ideas are generated, creative solutions are explored, and adaptability to change is embraced.

Having a culture of curiosity can positively impact an organization in several ways:

- Innovation: Curiosity can lead to the exploration of new ideas, technologies, and methods, fostering innovation within the organization.

- Problem solving: Curious individuals are more likely to seek out solutions and alternative approaches to challenges, driving effective problem solving.

- Learning and development: A culture of curiosity encourages continuous learning and development as individuals and teams seek to expand their knowledge and skills.

- Engagement: Curious employees are often more engaged with their work, as they are naturally motivated to explore and understand their tasks and projects.

- Adaptability: Curiosity enables individuals and teams to adapt to changing circumstances and market conditions, helping the organization stay relevant and competitive.

- Collaboration: Curiosity can facilitate collaboration and knowledge-sharing among employees as they seek to learn from each other's experiences and expertise.

To fully benefit from a curiosity-driven culture, organizations should foster an environment that encourages and rewards curiosity. This can be achieved through various means, such as providing opportunities for learning and exploration, recognizing and celebrating innovative ideas, and creating a safe space for experimentation and failure. It's important to note that while the Curiosity Curve assessment can provide valuable insights, it should be complemented with other approaches, such as open communication channels, brainstorming sessions, and idea-sharing platforms, to truly cultivate and harness the power of curiosity within an organization. Additionally, regular feedback and follow-up actions are based on the assessment results.

Dr. Debra Clary. All Rights Reserved 2023
debra@debraclary.com
Debraclary.com
502.435.5644

APPENDIX 2

hen you're starting a new leadership position, your first ninety days are crucial to your success. This ninety-day plan will help set you up for the success you envision:

Pattie Dale Tye Ninety-Day Plan Example

I. PDT prework: Read all I can to help me assess the current state, current assets, current trouble spots, customer requirements and expectations

    A. Prior-year financials, current-year financials

    B. Quality reports

    C. Business plans

    D. Customer satisfaction surveys

    E. Team's end-of-year appraisals, yearly quarterly accomplishments

    F. Yearly presentations to the board of directors or leadership team

II. Discovery first thirty days: Learn from the team, the customers, the process/operations outputs

    A. Run the business—first thirty days

       Listen and learn from the team: What are our thirty-, sixty-, ninety-day deliverables?

      1. Detailed view of ongoing business operations by department

      2. Department leadership presentations: goals, metrics, action plans

      3. Are there critical action plans needed to develop and implement?

      4. Who are our customers and partners?

         a) Patients

         b) Referring hospitals

         c) Physician groups / physicians

         d) Health partners / leadership / board of directors

         e) State of HHS?

         f) Federal government / CMS

         g) Fellow associates / teammates

         h) Community organizations

         i) Local government

         j) Health plans

5. For each customer/partner, what are we expected to deliver to meet their needs? What is our value proposition?

6. For each customer, what are we delivering? What metrics? Are they improving or deteriorating?

B. Understand the current-state view of our customers' perceptions (sixty to ninety days)

C. Listen and learn from the customers listed above

1. Internal documentation

2. Meetings with leadership for introductions to customers outlined above

3. Individual team member meetings/one-on-ones

D. What are our assets?

1. Leadership/people/team

2. Processes

3. Current referring hospitals / physicians

4. Relationships with others (regulators, etc.)

E. What are our growth opportunities?

1. New offerings

2. Competitive disruption

F. Gap analysis: Where are we missing customer and/or business expectations? Where are we underdeploying assets, and why? What are our underperforming assets, and what are the plans to remedy?

III. First draft of a 90-, 120-, 180-day business plan due to leadership

IV. Implement a method for routine updates/accountability readouts for the business plan

    a) Weekly executive leadership meetings

    b) End-of-month half-day leadership meetings

    c) Quarterly all-team meeting with action plan readout and celebration of results

    d) Biannual all-day business planning offsite

    e) Quarterly associate/team assessment

    f) Quarterly customer satisfaction assessment

Pattie Dale Tye brings a wealth of experience to this conversation with thirty-plus years of P&L leadership, including public/private start-up and turnaround business models. She successfully led businesses through regulatory evolutions such as the Affordable Care Act, Medicare Prescription Drug, Improvement, and Modernization Act, and the Telecommunications Consumer Protection Act. Using technology, new distribution channels, and innovative operational changes, she was able to reposition businesses and markets for success under new models of operating (telehealth, digital wellness, in-home monitoring, community advisory boards).

Pattie Dale was the president of two of the largest Texas insurance markets during her career with Louisville, Kentucky–based Humana Inc. During her career, she successfully turned around Humana's large business segment, realigning the pricing/profit model with the value proposition and rebuilding the brand and service reputation at a local market level. Early in her career, her leadership at AT&T centered around telecommunications and technology delivered to large-scale customer contact centers.

Always a believer in giving back to the communities she works and lives in, Pattie Dale helped increase Humana's visibility in Texas by engaging in activities that helped address broader health and wellness issues, such as Houston's Corporate Games, the American Heart Association's Heartwalk and Go Red for Women campaigns, and the United Way, among other philanthropic activities. She was also the president of Baylor College of Medicine's Baylor Research Advocates for Student Scientists, which provides scholarships and research funding to promising young biomedical research scientists. Later, Pattie Dale was able to take this spirit of giving back while moving forward to a national level, with her work leading Humana's Bold Goal.

Contact

To connect with Pattie Dale, please visit www.pattiedaletye.com.

ENDNOTES

1 Meg Jay, *The Defining Decade: Why Your Twenties Matter and How to Make the Most of Them Now* (New York, NY: Twelve, 2021).

2 Philippians 2:4, paraphrased.

3 "Carly Fiorina," Wikipedia, September 17, 2023, https://en.wikipedia.org/wiki/Carly_Fiorina.

4 Ibid.

5 "Discernment," Wikipedia, March 27, https://en.wikipedia.org/wiki/Discernment#:~:text=Discernment%20is%20the%20ability%20to,are%20not%20obvious%20or%20straightforward.

6 "What Is the Highlands Ability Battery (HAB) Assessment?" The Highlands Company, August 15, 2023, https://www.highlandsco.com/whats-highlands-ability-battery.

7 Johnson O'Connor, "Aptitude Testing and Research for College and Career Guidance," Johnson O'Connor Research Foundation, September 14, 2023, https://www.jocrf.org/.

8   "Free Personality Test, Type Descriptions, Relationship and Career Advice," 16Personalities, accessed September 20, 2023, https://www.16personalities.com/.

9   Gallup, Inc., "CliftonStrengths," Gallup.com, August 24, 2023, https://www.gallup.com/cliftonstrengths/en/252137/home.aspx.

10   In the third stage of your career, you are not ready to retire but rather ready to work your own pace, still contributing, learning, and leading.

11   See Luke 6:38.

12   Michael Watkins, *The First 90 Days: Critical Success Strategies for New Leaders at All Levels* (Boston: Harvard Business Review Press, 2003).

13   Martin Luther King Jr., "Remaining Awake Through a Great Revolution," speech, National Cathedral, Washington, DC, March 31, 1968, Martin Luther King, Jr. Research and Education Institute, https://kinginstitute.stanford.edu/king-papers/documents/remaining-awake-through-great-revolution-0.

14   Michael Hyatt, *Living Forward: A Proven Plan to Stop Drifting and Get the Life You Want* (Ada, MI: Baker Publishing Group, 2016).

15   "What Is Interoceptive Awareness?" Jane Taylor | Transition and Wellbeing Coaching | Life Coaching | Gold Coast, October 3, 2022.

16   Rodger Dean Duncan, "The Speed of Trust: It's a Learnable Skill," *Forbes*, July 18, 2018, https://www.forbes.com/sites/rodgerdeanduncan/2018/07/12/the-speed-of-trust-its-a-learnable-skill/?sh=31752 9613bbf%2C+Roger+Dean+Duncan%2C+contributor%2C+July %2C+2018.

17   "The Importance of Trust in Business," Behler Young, accessed September 20, 2023, https://www.behler-young.com/tech-tips/business-tips/the-importance-of-trust-in-business.

18 "Doing well by doing good—realizing the responsibility to give back to society—is a guiding principle and strategic plan of both progressive startups around the world and established businesses such as Starbucks, Land's End, Ben and Jerry's, and Whole Foods," excerpted from "Doing Well by Doing Good," *Harbert Magazine*, Auburn University, Harbert College of Business, https://harbertmagazine.auburn.edu/2018/03/21/ doing-well-by-doing-good/#:~:text=Doing%20well%20by%20 doing%20good%E2%80%94realizing%20the%20responsibility%20 to%20give,and%20Jerry's%2C%20and%20Whole%20Foods.

19 *Learning curve* definition in American English | *Collins English Dictionary*, accessed September 20, 2023. https://www.collinsdictionary.com/ us/dictionary/english/learning-curve.

20 Malcolm Gladwell, *Outliers: The Story of Success* (New York: Little, Brown and Company, 2008).

21 "Book Summary: Start with Why, by Simon Sinek." Sam Thomas Davies, March 20, 2023, https://www.samuelthomasdavies.com/ book-summaries/business/start-with-why/.

22 The word *others* refers to individuals who are neither clear on why they are in their current role nor have any idea where they want their careers to go or what path to take to achieve their goals. To stand out, you must know and act upon your why.

23 See Appendix 1 for an example of one of my ninety-day plans.

24 "The First 90 Days: Critical Success Strategies for New Leaders at All Levels," Mentorist, accessed September 20, 2023, https://www. mentorist.app/books/the-first-90-days-critical-success-strategies-for- new-leaders-at-all-levels.

25 Ibid.

26 I recommend reading *7 Habits of Highly Successful People*, by Stephen Covey. Habit 2 is "Begin with the End in Mind."

27 Chris McChesney, Sean Covey, and Jim Huling, *The 4 Disciplines of Execution: Achieving Your Wildly Important Goals* (Washington, DC: Free Press, 2012).

28 Ken Coleman, "6 Things That'll Improve Your Reputation at Work," LinkedIn Learning blog, accessed January 19, 2024, https://www.linkedin.com/business/learning/blog/career-success-tips/6-things-that-ll-improve-your-reputation-at-work.

29 Stephen R. Covey, *The 7 Habits of Highly Effective People: Powerful Lessons in Personal Change* (New York: Simon & Schuster, 1989).

30 Arlin Cuncic, MA, "How to Stop Feeling like an Outsider When You Have Social Anxiety," Verywell Mind, May 22, 2023, https://www.verywell-mind.com/imposter-syndrome-and-social-anxiety-disorder-4156469.

31 Ibid.

32 A great acronym for the word fear (F.E.A.R.) is "False Evidence Appearing Real."

33 Rebecca Fraser-Thill, "How to Handle Imposter Syndrome to Be More Effective at Work," *Forbes*, December 15, 2022, https://www.forbes.com/sites/rebeccafraserthill/2022/12/13/how-to-handle-imposter-syndrome-to-be-more-effective-at-work/?sh=26d3d5152b43.

34 Kathy Caprino, "Impostor Syndrome Prevalence in Professional Women and How to Overcome It," *Forbes*, October 12, 2022, https://www.forbes.com/sites/kathycaprino/2020/10/22/impostor-syndrome-prevalence-in-professional-women-face-and-how-to-overcome-it/?sh=6862b5cd73cb.

35 Dock David Treece, "Are You in the Top 1%?" *Forbes*, June 8, 2023, https://www.forbes.com/advisor/investing/financial-advisor/are-you-in-the-top-1-percent/.

36   Godfrey Neale, financial literacy expert, "Are You Rich? U.S. Wealth Percentiles Might Provide Answers," Kiplinger.com, August 12, 2022, https://www.kiplinger.com/personal-finance/605075/are-you-rich#:~:text=People%20with%20the%20top%201,The%20top%205%25%20had%20%241%2C030%2C000.

37   Lauren Schwahn, "Average Net Worth by Age: How Do You Compare?" Nerd Wallet, October, 27, 2023, https://www.nerdwallet.com/article/finance/average-net-worth-by-age.

38   "Three moves out" means that you are focused on the long term by developing new skills and gaining new education and experience that will benefit you in the long run.

39   The acronym F.O.M.O. can be used when describing "The Fear of Missing Out."

40   Malcolm Gladwell, "Outliers: The Story of Success," Amazon, 2019, https://www.amazon.com/Outliers-Story-Success-Malcolm-Gladwell/dp/0316017930.

41   Bernhard Schroeder, "Utilize These Six Steps to Become an Expert and Potentially Accelerate Your Career," *Forbes*, April 9, 2019, https://www.forbes.com/sites/bernhardschroeder/2019/04/09/utilize-these-six-steps-to-become-an-expert-and-potentially-accelerate-your-career/?sh=5388cc157f12.

42   Ibid.

43   "How to Build a Career You Won't Hate," *Harvard Business Review*, July 27, 2023, https://hbr.org/2022/02/how-to-build-a-career-you-wont-hate.

44   Ibid.

45   See appendix 3 for definitions and examples.

46   "How to Beat the Sunday Scaries," Headspace, accessed September 20, 2023, https://www.headspace.com/articles/sunday-anxiety.

47   See 1 Peter 5:7.

48   Reviewed by Lily Ramsey, "Serious Heart Attacks More Likely to Happen on a Monday," News Medical Life Sciences, June 5, 2023, https://www.news-medical.net/news/20230604/Serious-heart-attacks-more-likely-to-happen-on-a-Monday.aspx.

49   Up to 90 percent of corporate America takes Sunday off. But whatever day your "Sunday" is, be sure to unplug!

50   Ibid.

51   Julie Morgenstern, *Never Check E-Mail in the Morning: And Other Unexpected Strategies for Making Your Work Life Work* (Amazon, 2005), https://www.amazon.com/Never-Check-Mail-Morning-Unexpected/dp/0743250885.

52   Richard Carlson, PhD, *Don't Sweat the Small Stuff* (New York: Hyperion, 1998).

53   A great tool to use is the Eisenhower Matrix.

54   Karen McCullough, http://karenmccullough.com/.

55   "Taiki Matsuura Quotes," Goodreads, accessed September 20, 2023, https://www.goodreads.com/author/quotes/20861839. Taiki_Matsuura.

56   "Self-Discipline Definition & Meaning," *Merriam-Webster*, accessed September 20, 2023, https://www.merriam-webster.com/dictionary/self-discipline.

57   "Self-Discipline: Definition, Tips, & How to Develop It," The Berkeley Well-Being Institute, accessed September 20, 2023, https://www. berkeleywellbeing.com/self-discipline.html.

58   Alexander Pope, "An Essay on Criticism," pt. 2, line 525, in *The Poems of Alexander Pope*, ed. John Butt (New Haven: Yale University Press, 1963), 143..

59   "Overview," NASA, July 7, 2021, https://mars.nasa.gov/msl/mission/ overview.

60   See Appendix 1 for a detailed understanding of the Curiosity Curve.

61   "Curiosity Curve," website of Dr. Deb Clary, accessed September 20, 2023, https://debraclary.com/curiosity-curve.

62   Alinda Gupta, "What Is Corporate Athlete and Why Is It Important?" *Jumpstart*, September 17, 2021, https://www.jumpstartmag.com/ what-is-corporate-athlete-and-why-is-it-important.

63   Ibid.

64   "Weeble," Wikipedia, August 23, 2023, https://en.wikipedia.org/wiki/ Weeble.

65   "Martin Charnin," Wikipedia, August 24, 2023, https://en.wikipedia. org/wiki/Martin_Charnin.

66   Humana's Bold Goal "was established in 2015 with an aspirational goal to improve the health of the communities we serve 20 percent by 2020," accessed August 8, 2023, https://healthequity.humana. com/2020-bold-goal-progress-report/. For more information, visit https://www.humana.com/about/impact/community.

67 For a deeper look at ways to become more prevalent at work, I recommend reading *The 6 Types of Working Genius: A Better Way to Understand Your Gifts, Your Frustrations, and Your Team*, by Patrick M. Lencioni.

68 Skye Schooley, "What Is Thought Leadership, and Why Does It Matter?" accessed August 13, 2023, www.businessnewsdaily.com. https://www.businessnewsdaily.com/9253-thought-leadership.html. Updated April 11, 2023.

69 "What Is Thought Leadership?," WGU Insights Blog, Western Governors University, August 8, 2012, https://www.wgu.edu/blog/what-thought-leadership2012.html#close, accessed August 8, 2023.

70 "Go Red for Women," American Heart Association, accessed September 20, 2023, https://www.goredforwomen.org/.

71 "What Is Servant Leadership?" Greenleaf Center for Servant Leadership, accessed September 20, 2023, https://www.greenleaf.org/what-is-servant-leadership/.

72 Sarah K. White, "What Is Servant Leadership? A Philosophy for People-First Leadership," SHRM Executive Network, February 28, 2022, https://www.shrm.org/executive/resources/articles/pages/servant-leadership-.aspx, accessed August 30, 2023.

73 "Albert Mehrabian," The British Library, accessed August 30, 2023, https://www.bl.uk/people/albert-mehrabian.

74 Richard Petty (co-author), "Study: Body Posture Affects Confidence in Your Own Thoughts," August 2, 2009, https://news.osu.edu/study--body-posture-affects-confidence-in-your-own-thoughts/#pp-main, accessed August 30, 2023.

75 See Ecclesiastes 4:12.